THE BOOK OF WITNESSES

David Kossoff was born in London in 1919. After a short career as a furniture designer he began to devote his full time to acting, and soon became established as a familiar character actor (he has been playing men in their mid-sixties since he was in his twenties). A chance reading on the BBC of his version of a Bible story proved an astounding success, resulting in a series and his first book, *Bible Stories*. Subsequently he began a new radio series, *From the Book of Witnesses*, and requests came streaming in for copies of a book that was not yet written. *The Book of Witnesses* was an instant success in hardback, and is now available for the first time in paperback. David Kossoff lives in Hatfield with his wife, Jennie. They have two grown-up sons.

by the same author in Fount Paperbacks

BIBLE STORIES

THE BOOK OF
WITNESSES

David Kossoff

Collins

FOUNT PAPERBACKS

First published by Wm. Collins Sons & Co Ltd, 1971
First issued in Fontana Books, 1974
Second Impression November 1974
Third Impression June 1975
Fourth Impression May 1977
Reprinted in Fount Paperbacks June 1978
Sixth Impression June 1979

© David Kossoff 1971

Made and printed in Great Britain by
William Collins Sons & Co Ltd, Glasgow

This book is for my father, who died long ago. Once, when I was small, about eight, I was with my father, who was a loving man, in a narrow street in the East End. A huge labourer suddenly roared down at us that we had killed Jesus. My father asked him why he was so unhappy, and the fist lowered and the shouting stopped and he began to cry. We took him with us to my aunt for tea. This book is for my father, who was a loving man.

Contents

THE BABY

THE GROWING UP

CONTENTS

CONTENTS

THE BEGINNING OF THE END

9

CONTENTS

THE BOOK OF WITNESSES

How, you might ask, does a Jewish actor come to be writing a book all about Jesus? Not a very devout or scholarly or deeply-observing Jew; more a 'well-known', 'known to be', 'he's never denied it' sort of Jew. An occasional writer-and-teller-of-Bible-stories Jew. *Old* Testament stories. Of course.

Well, we live in many-media times. Occasional little stories become series; on radio and television. They become records, and short films – and are published. And an actor who wrote a little as a second string finds himself the author of a best-seller.

The bestseller contained all his stories but one. That one, from the New Testament, was an early, toe-in-the-water effort to solve a problem, to see how it came out. The problem was to find a format that would give him the same 'at home and at ease' feeling in the New as in the Old Testament. The little story told of three donkeys in Heaven reminiscing about their lives, in Jerusalem and Nazareth, long ago. What they saw, what they witnessed. Witnesses; there at that time.

Bestsellers, as in the way of things, demand sequels – and what other sequel can there be to the Old Testament but the New? The actor's reaction was as expected: 'But I am Jewish!' He became expert at evasive conversation on the subject. Promises were at last extracted from him that 'thinking about it' would take place. The thinking had a familiar shape. How to find a formula that would allow the same 'easy-walking' feel of the bestselling collection. A lot of reading was done; a lot of tryout writing; a lot of talking to priests. A trip to Galilee; a lot of walking and thinking in Nazareth. A problem, a problem.

The solution was right under his nose. The three donkeys. Witnesses. There at the time. But not donkeys, people. Faces in the crowd. People who were there; who *must* have been there. The worry stopped, the imagination raced, the pen flew. *The Book of Witnesses* was born.

As with the Old so with the New. From the first work on the book, a short radio series: *From the Book of Witnesses*. And from the first broadcast, no further doubts. The letters poured in, all wanting to know more about a book that did not yet exist.

Here is the book. A little description of each Witness heads each story. If, good reader, the description does not seem to match the way of the words, then make up your own description, attach a different person. No offence will be taken; the speakers are long dead.

Alternatively, if the way of the words bothers you, the way the Witnesses 'say it', do not be too concerned. Truth is not lessened by being spoken in translation.

Lastly, if it distresses you that the Witnesses of the book are fictional – and it cannot be denied – take comfort. At least that of which they speak is true. It is Gospel.

The Baby

•••••••••••••••••••••••••••••••••••••

SIMON

Ex-Temple worker. Now much engaged in youth welfare work. Middle fifties. Heavily built, with a ruddy complexion and greying hair. Blue eyes, rather bald. A smiling, pleasant man. A warm, kindly voice.

I was very fond of Zacharias. He was quite a bit older than me. When I was first taken on at the Temple he'd been there many years. The Great Temple in Jerusalem employed hundreds. All sorts of people, but for the jobs and duties connected with services and the inner holy rooms and courts they were very selective. You had to be of a priestly family. And old Zacharias was. His family went right back to Abyah, a priest appointed by King David himself. The direct line of Aaron. Zacharias's wife, old Elizabeth, was also of that line. She was as nice and as kind to me as he was. I saw her often, and him every day. For a time I lived with them, they treated me like a son. They'd never had children of their own, it was their one sadness. So I sort of filled a gap. They loved children. Elizabeth used to help at the children's Scripture school, and when she used to tell the story of Abraham's wife, old Sarah, who laughed when the angel told her she would be a mother, Elizabeth would laugh too, rather sadly.

But when she became a mother, like old Sarah, in old age, she didn't laugh. She was full of gratitude. 'Simon,' she said to me, 'God is very kind. I was always a bit ashamed of being childless – and people used to say some very thoughtless and humiliating things – but now all that's over. My son is from God.'

'From God,' was true. Although poor Zacharias was stricken

dumb for nearly a year. A most remarkable time altogether. I remember very well when the dumbness began. We were in the Temple, during a service, and Zacharias had to go into the inner room where the incense altar was. The preparing and lighting of incense was one of his jobs. He was gone longer than usual and I went to see if anything was wrong. As I got to the door he came out. He was pale and trembling and couldn't speak. He kept making signs that no one could understand. I took him home and Elizabeth made him go to bed. When he was calmer he wrote it all down for us. He'd seen a vision, an angel, Gabriel himself, who'd told him that Elizabeth would have a son, who would be special and holy and a prophet, and who would prepare the way for the coming of the Lord – although we didn't know what the last bit meant till years after. 'And,' wrote poor Zacharias, 'when Gabriel had told me all this I expressed some doubts, so Gabriel said I'd better not say another word till it had all come true. And he made sure I couldn't.'

Poor Zacharias. But Elizabeth had no doubts at all. Soon she was pregnant. She didn't go out. She became calm and quiet, and sort of beautiful. She was far from young but she'd always been good-looking and she became beautiful. Zacharias looked at her with wonder in his eyes. Quite dumb he was. Not a sound. He was very gentle and thoughtful to her. He asked me to find a young woman to take over the housework and be company for Elizabeth and I wrote to my mother who found Ruth in the next village and she came down and took over my room. And me. She's my wife, and she can add to this story, if you want. It is, after all, rather a woman's story, and she has a remarkable memory, has Ruth.

Where was I? Yes, Zacharias. Well, dumb or not, father-to-be or not, his life didn't change much. He was not ill or anything and was back at work no more than a week after losing his voice. I was his assistant, he'd trained me, and we did not need words. The time passed very quickly. In a way, I think Zacharias got used to being dumb.

He got his speech back in a nice way. When Elizabeth's

time came she had a fine, healthy boy, with no trouble. She and Zacharias were much liked, and the crowds of friends and relatives made it a joyous occasion. I got carried away and proposed to Ruth. So did she, and accepted me. On the eighth day, as the child was fit and well, he was circumcised and given his name. It was pretty well understood by everybody that the boy would be called Zacharias, after his father. But at the moment in the ceremony when the name is given, Elizabeth said, 'No! He is to be called John.' Great disturbance; for there were no Johns in either family. Then they asked Zacharias, who asked for a writing-tablet. He stood next to Elizabeth and looked into her eyes. Two old people. Then he wrote: 'John is his name.' Everybody was very surprised. Nearly a family row. Then Zacharias *said* loudly and clearly, 'John is his name.' Nice moment. He was a remarkable child, that John. He became a preacher who believed in purification by water. In baptism. He became famous. He was called John the Baptist. I'll go and call Ruth.

RUTH

Rather like her husband. Big-boned and handsome. Black hair and eyes. Early fifties. A relaxed, easy person, quick to smile, and of great charm. Down-to-earth, sensible.

Of course, it's all a long time ago now and Jesus is dead, poor soul, and so is John. People are inclined, I think, to forget the parents of famous men. John's parents have both been dead for many years and hardly anybody ever mentions them. They only had John, and he never married, so they are forgotten. Not by me, they were two of the loveliest people I shall ever know. Kindness itself. John was a present from God, and God doesn't give presents to just anybody.

You know, when I tell people about them, I rather gloss over the fact that old Elizabeth, bless her sweet memory, had a baby at an age that everyone knows is out of the question for having babies. But she did, I assure you. I was there when the child was christened and called John – and Zacharias got his speech back. A remarkable occasion in every way. As Simon no doubt told you. I always thought that it was a bit harsh for the Angel Gabriel to strike the old man dumb, just because he couldn't quite believe the news that he was going to be a father. Maybe Gabriel didn't want Zacharias to go telling everyone.

You know, there was a happening during Elizabeth's pregnancy that stays in my mind most clearly. I was living with the old couple. My own home was far to the north, and, shortly after I'd joined them, they found a little house up in the hills so that Elizabeth could be quiet and secluded and hide herself away a bit. She was a bit shy about the whole thing. Very nice house it was, practical and pleasant. They'd no children and I was made very welcome. It was rough on Zacharias to be made dumb, for he liked to talk. But he could write and we managed. Elizabeth passed her days in a sort of dreamy happiness. She would tell me over and over again of how Gabriel had appeared to Zacharias in the Temple and told him about the son he was going to have. A holy, special son, beloved of God. She never tired of telling the story and I never tired of listening to her. She was full of wonder, like a child. 'Ruth,' she would say to me, 'imagine! I am picked out, chosen, blessed among women!'

Well, when she was about half-way through her pregnancy or perhaps a little more, we had a visit from a young relative of Elizabeth's. A young woman from Nazareth. I'd heard her spoken of but had never seen her. She was unmarried but engaged to a carpenter. He was not with her; she came alone. Elizabeth was pleased to see her, she'd seen almost no one since the baby had begun. The young woman's name was Mary, a quietly-spoken, friendly-faced person. We'd had no message that she was coming and Elizabeth was curious to see the young woman's reaction to her old aunt's rather surprising condition. But Mary had her own surprise. 'I know about it,' she said, 'the Angel Gabriel told me!' And she went on to tell us that the angel had told her that she, too, was to have a special, holy baby. When she'd pointed out modestly that she was not even married the angel had said that her husband-to-be, Joseph, would not have anything to do with the matter. God would be the father. The baby, a boy, was to be called Jesus and he would be a great man and his name live for ever.

When Mary had finished telling all this, Elizabeth became very excited. She laughed and cried and seemed full of joy. For the younger woman and also for herself. As she had perfect faith in her own promised child, she had the same faith in Mary's. She recalled that Gabriel had told her that her baby would be a prophet, to 'prepare the way', he'd said, 'for the coming of the Lord.' Neither she nor Zacharias had really understood that part but now she did. 'Ruth,' she said to me, 'Mary's baby is the Lord! I'm certain of it!' She was full of humility. She felt honoured that the mother chosen for the Lord should come to see *her*. Very typical of Elizabeth, that was. 'Ruth,' she said, 'even the baby inside me is full of joy at the news. He kicks and leaps and moves!' She made Mary and me feel, and it was true. We put our hands on her and she put her hands on ours. 'Be friends,' she said, 'love each other.' And we did. Mary and I are the same age. Then we were both girls in the middle of remarkable happenings. We became like sisters. Mary stayed about three months. She shared my room. We kept in touch for years.

John was a lovely baby. Good as gold. I looked after him until my own babies started to come. A lovely time in my life. I often think of it. Of Mary, and old Elizabeth, and of the love and happiness, and of their holy, special sons given by God, special men, born in glory, who died so terribly. Jesus and John the Baptist. One crucified and one beheaded. In their thirties. It's a great puzzle.

SETH

About seventy. A weather-beaten, ruddy, lined face. A still, patient man. Bent, but still wiry and active-looking. Blue eyes, of a sharp intelligence, but kindly and interested. A deep countryman's voice.

My father and my grandfather were shepherds. It is a thing that runs in families. My sons own their own farms and their own sheep, but that is progress. I always looked after other people's sheep. Mind you, my sons are both clever, and quick in the mind, like my wife. She's always been rather a scholar. A good thing, for I can hardly read or write, but that was not unusual when I was younger. We were looked down on, I suppose, for often we had to work every day, ignoring the Sabbath, and with so many priests among the people, we were often told we were breaking the law. Though where the priests would have got their perfect lambs for sacrifice without us, I don't know. They could be very rude, the priests. Especially the young, silly ones. It's the same today. And not just with priests. People speak before they think. That's one good thing about looking after sheep. You get into the habit of keeping quiet. If you have to use words, you take your time to get them right. Words are important.

People often tell me that mine was a dull life. Well, maybe. Looking after sheep *is* much the same each day. But many people have never seen the lambs play and leap, have never sat quiet on a hill and watched the sun. Or the moon. I like to watch the night sky, the moon and the stars. Once I saw, at night, a sight that very few have seen. Just once, but once was enough for any man. If a priest is rude to me, I always say to myself, 'It doesn't matter, I had that night and you didn't.'

I was about nineteen at the time, and, although it's now about fifty years ago, I remember it like yesterday. I lived with my parents, not far from Jerusalem, and I was one of a group of shepherds who looked after the sheep owned by the Temple. As I said, the sheep for the Temple services have to be perfect, and a great many are bred for food, too. We, our group, usually worked at night. On this night I'm talking about, we'd met up where we usually did, on the side of quite a big hill. We'd had a bite to eat and drink and were sitting talking. Around us, our hundreds of sheep. All normal and usual and quiet. Very restful and pleasant, those talks at night. It was a dark night.

Then there was a sort of stillness and a feeling of change, of difference. We all felt it. I had a friend called Simon, and he first noticed what the change was. It was the light. There was a sort of paleness. It was a dark night but suddenly it wasn't so dark. We began to see each other's faces very clearly in a sort of silvery shimmering light. We seemed surrounded and enclosed in a great glow. It was the purest light I ever saw. The sheep were white as snow. Then, as our eyes began to ache with it, just farther up the hill from us the glow seemed to intensify and take shape, and we saw a man. Like us but not like us. Taller, stiller. Though we were still enough, God knows.

He looked at us and we looked at him. We waited for him to speak. It didn't seem right (we all felt it) for any of us to speak first. He took his time – as though to find the right words – and then he began to tell us what he called good news of great joy. Of a new-born baby, born in David's town. A baby sent by God, to save the world, to change things, to make things better. He told us where to go and find the baby and how to recognize him. And to tell other people the good news. His own pleasure in telling us filled us with joy, too. We shared his pleasure – if you follow me. Then he stopped speaking and became two. Then four, then eight, and in a second there seemed to be a million like him. Right up the hill and on up into the sky. A million. And they sang to us. 'Glory to God,' they sang, 'and on earth peace to all men.' It was wonderful. It came to an end and then they were gone.

Every single one, and we felt lonely and lost.

Then Samuel, who was the eldest of us, said, 'Come, let us go and find the baby. David's town the angel said; Bethlehem. In a manger. In swaddling clothes.' And off we went. We ran, we sang, we shouted, we were important, we'd been chosen. We were special. We were on a search, we had to find a baby.

And we did find him. We were led there. There was no 'searching'. We were led, and we saw for ourselves. Not much to see, perhaps. A young mother and her husband and her newly born baby. Born in a stable because all the inns were full. Poor people they were. The man was a carpenter.

Well, we did as we'd been told, we spread the word, and people did get excited. But not for long. Nothing lasts. We shepherds were heroes for a while, but then everyone knew the story. It was old news. Soon we were just shepherds again. Doing a dull job. But we were different from all the rest. We'd had that night. I don't talk about it much any more. But it keeps me warm. I was there.

JETHRO

Over seventy. Of medium height and rather spare. The face is arresting. Very pale and thin-skinned with a gentle, almost saintly, expression, but with alert, bright brown eyes. The hair and beard are pure white and fine in texture. The voice is silvery, clear, precise. The hand gestures are graceful, small.

Sometimes people tell me that my life spent inside the Temple somehow has shut me off from the world outside. I explain that this is not so; that the world *out*side, as it were, comes *in*. Neither is the world *in*side an unchanging one, any more than the outside world is; many changes, many.

When Herod died and Archelaus was King, the terrible riots and massacres were *in Temple precincts*. When the Roman procurators came to Jerusalem, one after the other, always in the Temple we felt change! The tempo of life changed. Thirty, thirty-five years ago, life in the Temple was easier somehow. Just as orthodox, just as strict in the observances, but softer.

It was like a small town, a village. Very high walls, as somebody once said, but many gates. A wonderful feeling of shelter, of safety. A haven. As people grew old, they would try to live close to the Temple, and they would spend all their days within the walls. They had their place. They were honoured, shown great respect. At that time, just before Herod died, most of my work was in the part of the Temple where the old people sat, near the Inner Court where the babies were brought for the ceremony of Presentation to the Lord and the Blessing. It was pleasant to see the young parents and their babies and our 'old residents', as we called them, all together sharing the joy. Some of these were grand occasions, with large families bringing huge offerings of animals for sacrifice and gifts of every kind, but the kind I liked best were the poor people, who were allowed by the Law to bring as their gift a pair of young pigeons, or turtle-doves. Always shy, such young people, always overawed. And nearly always put at their ease by one or other of our 'old residents'.

Some of these old ones were famous. Two I remember very well. One, Anna, was said to be a prophetess. Very old indeed, very devout. She lived in the court of women. She had married young but had been widowed after only seven years. She gave her life to God soon after. When I first met her she must have been nearly eighty. A great quality of stillness, of repose. It was easy to believe that she could see into the future, that she knew more than others. But she was not remote. She was kind, and of a sympathetic nature. People confided in her. She was interested. A good listener. She knew all about her old friends; she'd been there longer than any of them. She knew them well. Often we would talk of another favourite of mine, Simeon, another very old resident. Like Anna, also surrounded by legend, also 'famous'. He, it was said, had been told by God that he would not die until he had seen and touched the Messiah, the saviour of Israel, the one given by God. Simeon was regarded as a bit of a joke by some of the other old ones, but not by Anna. 'Simeon is very old,' she said to me once, 'but he is close to God, and God knows him well. I sleep little,' she said, 'but lately I dream, and I think that soon I will lose my old friend Simeon.'

She would say no more, and I tried to put it from my mind, but I found I was making it my business to be near Simeon whenever I could. He liked to sit in the sun, 'looking at the people go by,' as he put it. I don't know quite what I expected. It could be anybody. He spoke to many, a friendly man. Apart from the young fathers, all sorts of people. Holy men and soothsayers and seers and prophets were no strangers in the Temple. All sorts of learned close-to-God teachers and preachers were constantly passing through.

So I watched carefully. Who Simeon met, and how he reacted. Well, I was there when it happened. When he met the one that would allow him to die happy. I shall never forget his face. The moment had come, the sign so long awaited. And yet, it was strange, when it came, it was at once astonishing and ordinary. You will understand better what I mean, if I tell you a little more about Simeon, and about myself, too.

I have worked in the Temple all my life. As my father did, and his father. I began when I was fifteen, and finishing my education within the Temple. The elders and teachers in the Temple were men of vast knowledge. My first duties were all to do with ritual, with the services and festivals. People came from all over the world to Jerusalem, to see Great Herod's Temple. A pilgrimage, a wonder. But soon I began to know the regulars, the members of the congregation who never missed. Every Sabbath, every feast, every fast. The devout.

And Simeon was one. I was about twenty when we first met. About fifty years ago. And he was elderly then. He was kind to me. I had much to learn, and he knew all the services by heart. He was a very highly respected man, and when we first met, much involved in community and charity work. He did less as the years passed, and spent more and more time in prayer and with the Scriptures. It was a great part of his life to join in the ceaseless discussion among the elders and the teachers on the hidden meanings in the great history books of the people. The writings of the prophets, the written-down visions of the sages and seers of long ago. He would meditate for hours, almost in a state of mystical trance — often during a long fast. As the years passed, he confided in me more and more. And one day — and this must be nearly forty years ago — he told me he was now sure that a saviour of Israel was expected. 'It is written,' he said, 'it is shown in the books. One will come anointed by God. A Messiah. A leader.' He was lit up by the thought. Well, he wasn't the first to express such wish-thoughts. At that time there was a great hunger in people for a new, simple way. A kinder way. Great Herod was a hard king. Life was harsh; full of rules and regulations which had crept into God's Laws, too. So I listened to Simeon and gave him respect, but he wasn't finished. 'It has also been shown to me,' he said, 'that I will not die until I have seen the one sent by God.' He said it quite simply. He had not been very well, and he was quite old, but there was a sort of positive strength in him. From then on he lived in a state of expectancy, waiting. At first he spoke only to me about this conviction he had, but then others heard of it and some thought that Simeon was now senile as well as old.

But one morning, about five or six years after his vision, he was in the Temple earlier than usual. It was about a month after Anna had spoken of her dreams. 'Today,' he said. 'It will be today. I have been told and I am ready.' He sat in his usual seat. Near the Inner Court where the parents brought their babies for the Presentation to the Lord ceremony. A weekly thing; part of my job. I watched carefully. Many of the young fathers and their brothers or friends were fine Godly-looking men. But Simeon sat on. Then a poorly dressed

couple approached. The woman rather younger than the man
and carrying her baby son. The man carrying the most modest
offering allowed by the Laws of Moses. A pair of doves.
Simeon got to his feet. He was trembling, and I went nearer
in case he should need help. He went forward, not as I
thought to bow low to the man, but gently to take the baby
in his arms. He stood and lifted his face and spoke to God,
as to a loving friend who'd kept a promise. He blessed God,
and thanked him. 'Now I can die in peace,' he said. 'I have
seen him – and held him in my arms.' He spoke on, of salvation, of a truth for all people, of a standard too high for
many, of one who would see into men's hearts, and bring to
many a great joy. Then he stopped and looked into the face
of the young mother. 'But not you,' he said, and tears came
into his eyes, 'for you a sword, to pierce your very soul.' The
young woman was transfixed, amazed. I don't think she'd
understood most of what he'd said. Neither had I.

Simeon blessed them all and they went away. Back to
Bethlehem. Simeon died soon after. I missed him.

NEZZAR

*Of Babylon. Dark, smooth-skinned, with curled beard.
About sixty, of a learned manner but without pedantry.
A gentle, soft voice. A habit of smiling at the recollection
before speaking of it. Graceful, well-kept hands.*

I never liked to travel much. One of my brothers was a
merchant and he travelled all his life. It was his livelihood,
his work. He had no choice. I think perhaps that this place,
where I was born and have always lived, has something to do
with my dislike of travelling. Babylon, on the mighty
Euphrates, has everything a man needs. I had no need to
travel. But once, only once, I went on a remarkable journey.
A long journey, a search. It is a long time ago, but I remember it as clear as if it were yesterday.

I was about thirty at the time, and I lived and worked in the home of a man nearly twice my age. I was a scribe, and had a certain skill with figures. My master was a scholar and astrologer. He had spent his life in the study of the planets and stars. It was part of his religion, of mine, too. He was famous. His family was old and among his forebears had been soothsayers to the Persian court, lawmakers to the Medes, men of prophecy and divination. He was a silent, large man – with deep-sunk eyes. Often he would not speak for days and then would dictate to me, or just talk, as though to think out loud; to sort the mind. For about three years, he had been studying the Scriptures and the religion of the Jews of Israel, far to the west. He admired them. 'A remarkable people,' he would say, 'with a remarkable history, all written down. A history full of prophets and prophecies. A people who seem to be waiting. For a saviour, a leader, a Messiah.' My master was in close touch with other scholars and astrologers like himself. He and they were of the tribe called Magi, or wise men. Philosophers, thinkers, men of influence. Teachers, they were, and priests.

Well, one day my master seemed rather excited. A friend of his from a place up north on the Tigris had been staying with us, and they had been deep in study and discussion for days. And up most of the nights studying the stars. 'Something is happening,' said my master, 'something big. A whole series of signs and prophecies seem to be forming a pattern. We have worked separately and apart – and our conclusions agree. In two days' time we will have a third opinion. Have a room prepared.' And in two days a third friend arrived. I knew him well. A big, friendly man. I met him at the gate. 'Hallo,' he said, 'where are they? There's something big going on. Don't unpack my bags, pack theirs. We have to stop looking at stars, we have to start following one!'

We started the very next night. There was a lot to arrange but the three of them were energetic and lively as schoolboys. They pointed out the star. 'A new one,' they said, with wonder, 'and it moves and gets brighter and we have found words and prophecies. We have to go and find a king and speak to him of another king greater than he, and we have to take for the greater king worthy presents. Gold and frankincense and myrrh. As the Queen of Sheba long ago took gifts to King Solomon, so we, too, have to go to Israel with gifts for a king!'

The caravan was big. Servants to put up tents, to cook, to look after the camels, and to guard the gifts – which were gorgeous. The purified resins of the frankincense and myrrh were in priceless caskets covered with jewels. I had never been outside the city, and suddenly I was faced with a journey of hundreds of miles across desert. I had duties. I was in charge of the gifts, the astrological tables, the books – and the Magi also. For wise men are notoriously bad at looking after themselves.

We went from East to West and by the time we got to Jerusalem my three wise men had worked it all out. The king we were looking for was not Great Herod, but a baby, a little child, recently born. And not a king of a country, but 'King of the Jews'.

Jerusalem was beautiful – and the Great Temple breathtaking. Equal to, if not better than, anything we had at home in Babylon. We began our inquiries and soon were aware of a strange atmosphere. The Magi were right, people did seem to be waiting for a leader, a king, an Anointed One, a Messiah. A feeling of expectancy, a hope, a waiting. In all kinds of people. But the people of Jerusalem were very careful in their replies.

'A new king?' they said. 'We have a king. Herod. And he has sons. And,' they said, 'Herod has murdered many to protect his throne, to ensure the succession.' 'Be cautious,' said an old priest, 'Herod is old and ill, and as sick in the mind as in the body. Be cautious, his people are everywhere.' And very soon, some of Herod's 'people' came, with an invitation from the King. I was nervous, but the Magi were not. 'The King was on our list of people to ask,' they said. 'We are not beggars. We are a tribe of priests, of teachers. In Persia we teach kings their job.'

And indeed Herod showed us great courtesy. I accompanied my master, the eldest of the three, as secretary and aide. The King asked many questions and seemed interested and helpful. He told us that his own priests and scribes had found in the Scriptures a prophecy that pointed to Bethlehem as the place where we would find the child. 'Go,' said Herod, 'find the child and send me news. So that I, too, can come and pay my respects.'

Bethlehem was not far, and that very night the great glowing star, which had led us all the way from Babylon, led us to a small house in a narrow street and we saw the child. A young mother, with a rather older husband. Poor people. I could see nothing remarkable, but my master and the other two Magi wept and prayed and handed over the gorgeous presents of gold and incense they had brought. The parents seemed rather stunned. The child slept. It was difficult to get the three wise men back to the inn and to bed. They were like excited children. In the middle of the night, my master woke me. His face was serious. 'Get up,' he said, 'rouse everyone. Pack everything and load the camels. All three of us have had the same dream. A clear message from God that we must not return to Herod but must go back to the East at once, by a different route. There is great danger. Come, hurry.' 'What about the child and his parents?' I said. 'If God goes to such trouble for us,' he said, 'three elderly Magi, we can be fairly certain that he will look after the little family. That is no ordinary child.'

Well, we escaped. We went back to Babylon. I don't know what happened to the little family. Herod died soon after and his sons reigned as part-kings under the Romans. And I never left Babylon again. And we never saw the great star again.

SHEM

*Late sixties, or early seventies. A tall, lean, sinewy man.
Deep-set eyes, which are dark and alive. Clean-shaven,
with close-cropped hair. The face is strong, the skin
weather-wrinkled and tanned. Big, worker's hands.*

I'm not a religious man, you understand, and I didn't have
much in the way of an education, but I'm not young and I've
travelled a lot and listened a lot and you learn, you know,
you learn. I was born in Samaria in the same year that Herod
became King. Herod the Great he was called. Well, maybe
he was great. He didn't do much for us in Samaria. All right,
we are a mixed lot but we are not lepers. Our law is based
on the same rules as the rest of Israel. The Law of Moses.
One of those Laws is that the children shouldn't suffer for
the sins of the fathers. That's a joke. All my life I've suffered
for some nonsense generations ago about my people wanting
to help in the rebuilding of the Great Temple and being
refused because our religion wasn't holy enough. You'd have
thought a few extra gods and idols would have made it *more*
religious. And Samaritans are good builders. My family have
been joiners and carpenters for a long time. I think that's
what first drew me to Joseph.

I'm a journeyman; I work anywhere. My tools are my
luggage. When I first met Joseph and his little family in
Bethlehem it was the first time I'd ever been there – and I've
worked all over; Phoenicia, Syria, Parthia, Egypt. Not a big
place, Bethlehem. One big inn, a decent synagogue, a meeting
hall. Anyway, this inn had been damaged by some sort of
religious demonstration. There'd been crowds of people who'd
broken things off for souvenirs. A lot of the timber in the
stables needed replacing. I heard about it and was taken on.
I found a room on the edge of the town. And met Joseph,
who lived next door. When he told me he was also a joiner,

I told him about the inn and he smiled and said he'd like to help with the repairs. So I put in a word for him and we worked together.

Very quiet man he was. His wife was younger. Her name was Mary. They had a baby boy. When I met them, they'd just come back from taking the baby to the Temple in Jerusalem for his blessing by the priests. Joseph and I worked together for some weeks before I told him I was a Samaritan. 'Oh,' he said, 'I've never been in Samaria. Will you eat with us this evening?'

Well, I forget now how long we worked at the inn but we got it done and I was working on a barn north of the town. I'd kept my room on and one night I got back very late. It was pay night and I like a drink. The street was quiet and dark. As I got ready for bed, Joseph knocked on my door. 'Can you help us?' he said, 'We have to leave right away.' We went next door. Mary was packing and the baby was fast asleep in his crib. On the table were three caskets. They were gorgeous. Gold they were, worth a fortune. 'Gold, frankincense, and myrrh,' said Joseph, 'gifts for the baby. They can bring death to us all. We have been told by God to go down to Egypt. Right away. Tonight. We know nothing of long journeys. Please help us.'

I went next door and packed my tools. We were out of the place in an hour. We borrowed a donkey for Mary to ride on with the baby and we joined a trade caravan of merchants and we kept ourselves to ourselves. If people got too inquisitive I used rough talk and said loudly I was a Samaritan. That got rid of them. Sins of the fathers can be very useful sometimes.

Now you might ask why did I go with them. Well, there was nothing heroic in it. I've moved around working in different places all my life. And Joseph had hardly been out of his town. Also we were both joiners, and carpenters can pick up work anywhere if you know the way. Another thing, as I told you, I'm a Samaritan, which at that time, thirty-five years ago, just before Great Herod died, was the same as being a leper nearly. No one had a good word for you. You walked by yourself. Well, Joseph was an orthodox Jew and he accepted me like a brother – and so did Mary. Even the baby liked me. I was one of the family. Of course I went with them. I looked after them.

It took us a long time to do the journey. We had a donkey for Mary and the baby, but Joseph and I walked. We stayed with no one long, for Joseph and Mary were afraid. My gentle friend, who never raised his voice, was a wanted man. Mad King Herod himself was after him. Well, not him so much as the baby. I don't know all the ins and outs of it even now, but somehow or other Joseph and Mary had got an early warning that Herod was going to kill all the baby boys under two in Bethlehem. They were not hysterical people, and when they went I went with them, but I didn't really believe such a thing would happen. But it did. We heard about it. Mary wept for days, and Joseph was quieter even than usual.

We didn't go deep into Egypt. We stayed this side of the great delta of the Nile and found a little house in a village. There was enough work round about and the village people were used to travellers. We weren't too far from the coast and a main trade route. I've made a point all my life not to ask too many questions. If people want to tell me something, they will. Joseph never spoke much. Once, when I said I'd no idea how he knew about the order to kill the babies, he said, 'I didn't know. I was told in a dream by an angel of God to leave immediately. My little son was given to Mary by God. I did as I was told.' He was quite serious. I made a sort of joke, I remember. I said, 'Well, when the angel tells us to go back home, let me know. I'm not too fond of Egypt.' Joseph laughed.

I forget now exactly how long we lived in the village but one morning I came down and Joseph had the little boy on his knee. Mary was by the stove, Joseph smiled. 'Good morning,' he said, 'we can go home.' 'Another angel?' I said. 'Same one,' said Joseph, 'Herod is dead. It is safe now.' Well, it wasn't so safe really. Herod's son, Archelaus, was now King and was more hated and more cruel than his father. There'd been riots and disturbances and mass executions, so when we'd gone up the coast as far as Gaza, Joseph decided that he would not go back to Bethlehem, where little Jesus had been born, but farther north to Galilee, where it was more peaceful. He knew Galilee, he came from Nazareth, and that is where we finished up. I went with them and helped them find a place and get it fixed up, but then I moved on. Nazareth was a very religious, very orthodox place. Joseph fitted in well, me not at all. I was sorry to go. I saw them from time to time. The last time I saw them, the eldest lad, Jesus, was getting ready to go to the Temple in Jerusalem for his confirmation. He was twelve or thirteen. Fine boy. Then I worked in Syria and Cyprus for a long time and lost touch. But I think of that time often.

SYLVANUS

Over seventy. A thin, pale, acid man. The skin of the face very fine and wrinkled, the eyes hooded, many-folded. The voice is meticulous, slow, rather high. The impression of frailty is physical only; the strength of mind is apparent immediately.

It may be that, when we have conversed for a little while, you will form the opinion that I am a cynic, or a sceptic. It is an opinion that you may well carry away with you. You will not be the first, and if we meet again, it may well prevent us being friends. Well, I shall understand. I have very few friends. As I get older (if getting much older is even possible in my case), I find I can do with fewer.

However, as to my being a cynic, or a sceptic, you must remember that I have spent my whole life at court. I have seen black proved white and miracles made commonplace. I have seen slaughter blessed by holy men and sanctity made a crime. I have seen prophets and men of God murdered with not a word from the God they represent. I have seen wickedness prevail and virtue made meaningless. I have watched vanity lift a man to heights where humility is unknown. So you will readily understand (I hope) that in such a world detachment can become an art; cynicism a protective shield; scepticism the only intelligent attitude.

My world was the world of Herod. King Herod. Herod the Great. And great he was. People, I find, when remembering others, remember the bad and forget the good. They remember Herod's senseless murders and forget his loving rebuilding of the Great Temple. They remember the stupidities at the end of his life and forget the far-sighted good sense at the beginning. He was a Jew who knew how to be a Roman and the Romans recognized his worth. Antony himself made Herod King. And Octavian, great Augustus Caesar, agreed.

You might say to me that Herod was mad. Possibly. But it was not a time of sanity and a certain madness is not unknown in great men. Also, it should be remembered, although it is difficult to believe, that Herod, Great Herod, never, ever, felt secure. He was suspicious, often rightly so, of everyone round him. Certainly he had little joy of his wife, the exquisite Mariamne. She was like ice. Admittedly, her life was, to say the least, difficult. When her younger brother, whom Herod had made a high priest, became popular, Herod had him drowned, in his bath. Her grandfather, of eighty-seven, was put to death. Her sons were killed. Handsome, well-liked young men, with their mother's looks. There was so much death. Even Mariamne herself was killed. Tragedy, tragedy. It almost turns into bizarre comedy the ghastly edict made by Herod that all boy babies under the age of two in Bethlehem should die to make certain that one particular baby was destroyed. This special baby that everybody seemed to be talking about.

Herod, being as I say a morbidly suspicious man, had built up, over the years, a very efficient informer system. At court we knew everything that went on in Judea. We knew about the crowd of shepherds looking for a baby born in a stable the morning after it had happened. We knew exactly how long the excitement would last; we'd had glad tidings from angels before. We'd had Messiahs by the dozen – and had regulations about how to get rid of them. Holy men and healers and miracle-makers and magicians were thick upon the ground.

A report was given to Herod about the baby in the stable but I don't think he even read it. He was quite ill at the time, and very unbalanced. He was full of disease, bloated, disgusting. He was in pain, living on drugs, but hardly sleeping at all. He was afraid of the dreams, I think. He looked awful.

He was nearly seventy and looked a hundred. He had ruled in one way or another since he was fifteen. He had killed without mercy. Enemies; friends; his own flesh and blood. His hands were red. It was said at court that remorse, about Mariamne and his dead sons, was destroying his mind. His periods of lucidity were infrequent. Reports about shepherds and special babies were unlikely to be read.

But not long after the shepherds, wise men from far-off places came to him, talking of a baby. Of a baby that was to be, so they said, 'King of the Jews'. They had seen signs, they said, a bright star, they said. And Great Herod, mighty king, was filled with a mad fear of a poor baby born in a stable, who was going to steal his kingdom. With a heavy and transparent cunning he told the wise men to find the child and bring him news so that he could do homage, prepare the way, make ready the throne.

He never saw the wise men again and he never found the baby. So he made the terrible order: 'Kill *all* the babies!' he said. 'All boy babies under two.' It was almost the last order he made. He was dead soon after. And never another word of the baby.

It is nearly forty years ago. Indeed I am old. I saw many changes after Herod, many. The country was divided among such sons as were still alive. Men of cruelty and folly and weakness. The worst, Archelaus, banished by the Romans after ten years, who would have no more kings of Judea. From then on, the country was run by procurators, who were Roman. I knew many. The one I remember most clearly was Pilate. Pontius Pilate.

Here Sylvanus stopped, saying he was tired, having been unwell recently. He said he would be happy to speak again another time. He kept his promise. On page 133.

The Growing Up

EZRA

About sixty. Small, silvery. A lined, intelligent face, with deep-sunk rather piercing eyes. An impression of neatness in both appearance and posture. A contained, still man. A clear, educated voice.

Although, as you say, Damascus is an important place on a main trade route, which means that Damascus knows quickly what has happened elsewhere, it does not necessarily follow that all who live here in Damascus are quite so well informed. The high wall enclosing this garden is no accident. Neither is the rather secluded position of my little house. I work at my own speed, in gold and silver and precious stones. I do not need the world shouting its news in my ear. I am not fond of the world, which shouts obscenities and is cruel. My friends are poets and painters and musicians, who call me, to my intense pleasure, artist. Not metalworker, or craftsman, but artist.

So, if you sit and tell me that a Galilean preacher, executed by crucifixion nearly a year ago, was the youngster I knew twenty years ago in Nazareth, I must believe you. You seem an honest man, and certainly the matter of the caskets is convincing.

I lived in Nazareth for about three years in all. I've lived in many places. My main repute for many years was as a restorer, a repairer, of jewellery and articles of gold and silver. I still do. To make things new again gives me as much pleasure as to make new things. So I could live anywhere, in small towns or great cities, fairly sure of making a good living.

My house in Nazareth was small but adequate for my

needs. I never married, and am well able to look after myself. The house was south of the market, in a street where a number of metalworkers lived. It was one of them, Samuel, who found me my house. It was also Samuel who brought me the casket. Samuel worked in iron and brass. Large work.

One day, not long after I'd moved in and set up my workshop, he visited me. We drank some wine and talked of this and that. Then he told me that a casket made of gold, inset with precious stones, had been brought to him for repair. Not his kind of work at all. He had explained to the woman and she had taken it away again.

'Woman?' I said. Samuel then went on to explain that the way the woman was dressed, simply, like a workman's wife, had also made him unwilling to touch the casket. 'Which was gorgeous,' he told me, 'Babylonian, or Armenian work. Superb, beyond price.'

I was curious. I sensed a mystery. I told Samuel to send the woman to me. He promised to do so if he saw her again, for she'd left no name. A week or two passed and then he told me he had been fitting a wrought screen in a house and the joiner doing the cupboards and windows was one day brought his lunch by the woman, who was his wife. Samuel had greeted her and mentioned my name.

Two or three days later she came to my house – with the casket. She had with her a boy, of about eleven years old. Her eldest son, she told me. He was good-looking, as she was. He resembled her. She carried the casket wrapped thickly in cloth. When I took off the cloth, it took my breath away. Quite superb. Worth a fortune. The woman listened to my rapture calmly. She was a calm, quiet person, with a look of great candour.

'Very few people have seen the box,' she told me. 'It was given to my son' (she put her hand on the boy's arm) 'shortly after he was born. By a wise man from far away who seemed to be very rich. There were three.'

'Three wise men?' I said.

'Yes,' she said, 'and three boxes. This one contains as you

see small blocks of pure frankincense resin.'

It did, too. Quite full. The purest, whitest, I'd ever seen. I asked her about the other boxes, as she called them.

'One is of pure gold, without jewels,' she said, 'and contains gold. The other is like this one and also contains blocks of resin. Of myrrh.' Then she paused. I remember it so clearly. 'Myrrh,' she said, 'which is used in the purification of women and the anointing of kings. It is used in wine to deaden pain. It is used in the preparation of the dead for the grave, and in the ointment of embalming.'

It was said strangely. Not to inform, to show knowledge, but in an even flat voice. Then, with more animation, she told me what she wanted done. To repair and make new again. The work I love. The workmanship of the casket was wondrous. I knew that, in putting right the damage here and there and in its renovation, I would learn much, and I made that my excuse for promising to do the work at a very low price. The woman, her name was Mary, I recall, told me that they had little money anyway, and that her plan was that her husband Joseph would pay me in work. He was a skilled carpenter, she told me, and they often paid bills that way. Also, she said, the boy would give his services in any useful way.

I found her honesty and simplicity most attractive, and agreed. And so it was. I worked on all three caskets and was paid in benches and shelves and cupboards – and a beautiful hardwood workbench, which I use to this day. And when the family took the boy to Jerusalem to be confirmed at the age of thirteen, I looked after the boxes for them.

He was a pleasant boy. We became good friends. I would see him nearly every day. He would call in to see me if I needed anything and I grew to trust him completely. A steady lad, with good sense, and initiative. His father was teaching him to work in wood and I added a few lessons in metalwork. He was quick and dexterous. He enjoyed the company of older people, I think. He always seemed a little apart with boys of his own age. He was a good reader and loved the Scriptures, as I do, so we had lots in common.

I left Nazareth about nine months after his confirmation in Jerusalem. I was sad to leave. I made him a belt buckle in silver and bronze with his name, Jesus, engraved on it. I went far away to the North, and later to the East, and I lost touch with the family. Pity.

It is very sad to think that a pleasant boy like that should have come to such an end. He could have been no more than thirty-three or -four. Awful. I wonder if Mary somehow knew (women, I'm told, are remarkable in such things); I wonder if she knew in some way that her pleasant son would die young, and have myrrh, the gift of his birth, used in the anointment of his death. Poor Mary. Sad, sad indeed.

ESHTOL

Early fifties. Tall, well-built, with a rather serious, scholarly expression. Grey hair and beard. The fore-finger used much in speech, tutor-like. A warm voice, and strong.

I was born here in Jerusalem, and have always lived here. I've never wanted to live anywhere else. My father used to say – well, he still does – 'Why leave Jerusalem to see the world? The world comes here to Jerusalem!' It's true. It is a place of infinite variety, a different mood each day, a different colour. The Jerusalemite can be cruel and kind, warm and cold, stubborn and easily led – like the people of a major city anywhere. The city has much to be proud of – and some things of which it may be ashamed.

Last year's business with the Galilean preacher, Jesus of Nazareth, is a happening many people would like to forget. I heard him preach a number of times. Remarkable. And in no way dangerous to law and order, I would have said. I was told he was a healer; he could cure disease and make the blind see. Certainly his followers work very hard to keep his memory and lessons alive. They will, I fear, get into the same trouble as their leader.

A friend of mine, a lawyer, told me that the preacher seemed to go out of his way to provoke the authorities, to make them angry, to make them look foolish. He gave offence, he ruffled feathers, he pricked pomposity in high places, he showed no respect for the Establishment. My friend says no wonder they killed him. And Jerusalem wept. And jeered. And stayed at home. And went in their thousands to the execution. Like people everywhere.

Perhaps, in its 'infinite variety', Jerusalem is best at the times of fast and feast. The festivals. Looking back – and I have played a small part in a great many such celebrations – I think I am right. I have always loved festival time. Passover, perhaps, more than all others.

Passover in Jerusalem was always, for me, full of beauty. I think the Temple had a lot to do with it. The gorgeous restoration by King Herod was one of the wonders of the world, and during the festivals a lot of extra people were taken on to help handle the huge crowds of extra worshippers and tourists. My family are of a priestly tribe and so I was eligible for these duties. But although of a priestly tribe, we were not priests, my father and I. We were both school-teachers, but at Passover time, more than at any of the other festivals, we *felt* like priests. We looked forward to it.

Such a happy festival, with the wonderful stories of Great Moses leading the slaves out of Egypt, and the miracles of the parted sea and food from Heaven and the sweet water from the rock. And the plagues and the terrible visit to Egypt of the Angel of Death, who passed over the Jewish homes. The passing over of the Angel. The Passover. Every year in the Great Temple the youngsters' eyes used to grow wide at the story of the Angel. There were always a lot of youngsters. And always among them boys of twelve or thirteen brought by their parents to be made 'a son of the Law', a man. A lovely part of the service. I taught boys of that age, and I knew what terrors they could be, but during that day in their lives they were angels. Spotless, obedient, glowing with pride.

It was part of my job to see that when each family left the Temple they paid a courtesy visit to Solomon's Colonnade, in the great courtyard, where the elders and teachers held their open-air discussions. The boys and their parents would listen dutifully for a while to the rabbis and theologians and then go away to their celebrations and more interesting things. All quite understood and allowed for. These discussions, on the fine points of the Scriptures and the Laws and the sayings of the prophets, were *not* of much interest to the children. It was grown-up talk.

Occasionally a boy, well prepared by his father or teacher, would ask a question, and listen, rather dizzily, to the learned answers, and then go away. But there was one boy, I remember, who didn't go away for nearly a week! It's about twenty years ago, but he stays in the mind, that boy. Nearly a week. My father and I and the old teachers and rabbis became fascinated by him. He was a good-looking well-built boy. He'd come as usual, after his confirmation, with his parents, to watch and listen. One of a number of families, all from Nazareth. They all left, but, not long after, the boy came back. He sat and listened, with great respect, which was usual, but with a remarkable comprehension, which was not. Even in grown-ups. You sort of felt this deep understanding, and when he asked a question, it showed. He would listen to the answer – and then discuss it! Which was unheard of! Boys *listened* to their elders; they did not *discuss*! And many of the old teachers on these occasions were rather lordly and conceited. But there was something about this boy. All day, every day, he was there. The old men looked forward to seeing him, they shared their food with him, enjoyed him. 'Little Rabbi' they called him; 'the Teacher from Nazareth'. The boy's knowledge of the Scriptures and of all the 'Messiah prophecies' was truly astonishing. He was articulate and his voice was pleasant on the ear. He had none of the awkwardness, or sullenness, or shyness that most boys of that age have with adults. He seemed almost to prefer grown-ups to youngsters of his own age. He had a very pleasant smile, and his laugh was infectious. I arranged for him to sleep at night in one of the junior students' hostels.

After about five or six days his parents came for him. We thought they'd known where he was, but it seems they hadn't. They'd searched everywhere. They'd left the city with all the other families of their party, and had nearly arrived back in Nazareth before they'd noticed that our boy was not among all the other lads. His mother was very upset and worried – and told him so. Very out-of-character behaviour on his part, we gathered. She and the boy were obviously very close. Quite a young woman, I remember. The father was a good bit older.

The boy listened to his mother and took his telling-off well. With dignity. He apologized, to both his parents, correctly. Then he said, rather oddly, I thought, 'Didn't you know I'd be here? In the Temple? In my Father's house?' Then he said goodbye to us and went away. The old men missed him, and were sharp and cross with each other for a day or two.

My father, who is quite old, but of unimpaired memory, is given much to what he calls 'conjecture thinking'. For about a month he has been convinced that the Galilean, Jesus, and our boy were the same person. It may be because Passover is coming round again – and we always recall the boy – or it may, in fact, be so. It would be dangerous, I think, at this time, to start to ask questions – and to no purpose. If it is so, as I said to my father, more's the pity.

ZIRIM

About forty. A tall, graceful man. Clean-shaven, with dark, luxuriant hair and delicate features. Finely shaped eyebrows and large, expressive eyes. The mouth and hands are feminine, the voice musical, and soft. Clothes, jewellery, and perfume, of great taste.

Since Jesus was crucified, six years ago, a hundred legends

and stories have grown up round him. Vast exaggerations
and 'eye-witness accounts' by people who never laid eyes on
him. A whole fellowship of followers and believers exists. To
every side, people who knew him and loved him.

I knew him. And loved him. And will do so till I die.
Which, believe me, is not so common here in Nazareth, where
he grew up. He was right; no man is a prophet in his own
town.

Most of the Fellowship, his followers and believers and
disciples, knew him for about three years. From the start of
his preaching and healing till his death. I knew him all his
life. We were the same age. We lived near each other. We
were boys together. At least, I say boys. Until I was about
six I didn't know what I was. I was an only child, and my
mother really wanted a girl, I think. So she dressed me like
a girl, and made my hair pretty and so on, and kept me
indoors, or in the garden. About the only outings I had were
to synagogue.

I hated going to synagogue. The children knew I was a boy
and they were very cruel. Not all of them. Not Jesus. One day
Jesus's father came to our house to do some joinery. To make
a cupboard in my bedroom. He thought I had a sister. When
I told him the room and the clothes and pretty things were
mine, he was surprised.

The next day he brought Jesus with him and we played in
the garden. Jesus was my first friend. He never laughed at me,
or called me names, or was cruel. The most elaborate and
detailed stories are told today of his tolerance and love for
others. Of his acceptance of people, no matter who they were,
whatever they'd done. Well, let me tell you he had those
qualities when he was six years old! Don't laugh at me,
friend, I tell the truth. There *are* such children, full of love,
and Jesus was one. Remember, I was a girl-boy, accepted by
neither girls nor boys. I needed someone to be my friend – and
to get me out of that garden – and to get my mother to change
my way of dress! Jesus did all three. He was my only friend.
Such 'boy' things as I did, I did with him.

My father had little time for me. He was a sport, an athlete. He wanted a son like himself, but was not strong enough to stop my mother's wanting me to be her daughter. He used to sneer and shout and bully. I hated him. He died of a seizure when I was nearly fourteen, about a year after Jesus and I had been to the Great Temple for our confirmation. To be made 'men in the eyes of God' as my old teacher used to put it. A poor joke in my case. I'm more woman than man – in anybody's eyes.

My father, as I said, died about a year later, and in the following year, at Passover time, Jesus asked me whether I would like to go with him to his aunt in Capernaum, on the Sea of Galilee, for a fishing and sailing holiday. My mother, who was still treating me like a child, wasn't keen, but Jesus's mother, Mary, talked her round.

It was the best holiday I ever had. We lived in the open. I don't know whether Jesus had told his aunt and uncle and cousins about me, but I was one of the family in about ten minutes. My clothes were too light, too gaily coloured (my mother to her dying day did not lose the habit), so I was given old stuff belonging to the cousins James and John. Jesus's aunt, Salome, told me to get as dirty and untidy as I liked, and stay that way – and then I'd be like *her* sons! She was marvellous to me. When I asked how I should address her husband, she said, 'Like everybody else does, just call him Zebedee!'

I got very brown and fit. James was a bit older than Jesus and I, and John a bit younger. They had just started in their father's fishing business, and Zebedee took Jesus and me on as extra hands, 'for bed, marvellous board, and not much money!' I can still hear him saying it.

There are few times in my life when I've felt like other men (most of the time I haven't wanted to), but I did on that holiday. I rose early, worked hard – and ate enough for three. After supper we would sing and drink wine till we were nearly asleep. Then to bed. A wonderful time. Wonderful.

I suppose, thinking about it, that on that holiday I became an adult, or whatever it's called. On that holiday James fell in love with a girl called Sara and later married her. On that holiday I fell in love too, I suppose. With Jesus. I don't know how else to put it. It was strange. For nearly ten years he had been my friend. My first and closest friend. My brother, my twin. I knew everything about him, as he did about me. Indeed, about my realization that I was more girl than boy, he alone knew.

I remember the moment. It is like a picture in my mind, a painting. We were about a mile off shore, in the smaller boat of the two Zebedee owned. It was a calm and beautiful day. We'd put our nets down and we were finishing our midday meal. There were just the four of us, and James was extolling the beauty and brains of his Sara. John was making ribald remarks, as brothers do, and Jesus and I were getting rather bored. Then James, who had little humour, got tongue-twisted and said something meaning quite the opposite of what he'd intended. I forget now what it was but we exploded. We lay back and we roared. James threatened us with a bucket of water but it made no difference. Then he looked at Jesus and began to laugh himself. Which was puzzling, for James hated to be laughed at. Well, it's difficult to explain, but Jesus was not laughing *at* James – John and I were laughing *at* him – Jesus was laughing, as freely as a child, because it was *funny*. His head was thrown back, his eyes were half closed against the sun, and his whole being was full of joy and happiness. He was naked to the waist, as we all were, and his skin was brown and smooth. His hair was long and untidy. I could draw how he looked.

The boat was full of laughter. Only I was silent. I wanted the moment to go on for ever. What is there like first love? I could hardly breathe. I was at once happier and more sad than ever in my life, before or since.

The moment passed, and everything was the same, and different. The holiday ended, and Jesus and I went back to Nazareth. I think my mother knew something had happened to me, we have always been very close, but I said nothing to anyone, certainly not to Jesus. I did not languish, or pine, or die for love. I saw my loved one nearly every day. He did not need to know. He had love for everyone, I loved only him. I was content. I did not have to disguise or change my ways, I was always affectionate and demonstrative, I had always admired him, had always said so.

The years passed, and when we were of an age to marry and neither of us did, the gossip started. I was by that time quite used to being called the various names for those of my kind. It was of no importance, there are many of us, but I did not want Jesus to be hurt in any way because we were friends. So my mother and I moved to Jerusalem. She raised no objection, indeed she was pleased to have her little boy to herself again. She never remarried, and we lived together until she died, about a year before Jesus did.

If you care for irony I can supply it. I am by profession an historian and teacher of history. At the time of Jesus's arrest and death I was teaching at the Pharisaical College and was also official recorder to Pilate. So, at the so-called trial of my childhood friend, I wore the badges of both Pharisee *and* Roman.

When Jesus died, I moved back here to Nazareth, to the house I grew up in. I have memories to last me a lifetime. I go for holidays to Capernaum. I have a little house there. And a boat.

REUBEN

Elderly, slight. A slow speaker, looking often for the right word. Educated and widely read. Born in Perea, living for most of his life in Jerusalem and, later, Nazareth. A bachelor, slightly spinsterish in his ways, but open and friendly.

It is difficult for me to believe, even after nearly two years, that Jesus is dead. Or that he brought about his own execution, or that he created such violent upheavals and disturbances. I knew him well, he was a pupil of mine. I taught him Scripture. Not when he was a child. When I came to live in Nazareth he would have been about thirteen or fourteen. He was the eldest of five brothers and two sisters, and a very responsible boy indeed. He had to be. A big family and not a great deal of money coming in. His father Joseph was a fine joiner, a good careful craftsman, but a one-man business. In busy times he would hire another pair of hands, but not often. He made all the furniture in this house, Joseph did, and the doors and cupboards, too. He married late. Mary was much younger than he was. She is still only in her middle years, although I hear she has aged a lot since Jesus died. They were very close always, she and Jesus.

I was a scribe and legal clerk for most of my working life, and taught Scripture in my spare time. Not so much for the money, but because I like children, and I come of a family of scholars. My father and grandfather were rabbis, and many of my uncles were teachers. But I have never had very good health, and neither the altitude nor the tempo of Jerusalem really suited me, so I gave up my legal work and moved my home here to Nazareth. Nearly twenty years ago now. I have never married and my needs are few, and, once I was accepted by the town, they found a place for me. I became a teacher in my own pleasant house, which, as you see, is only two doors away from where Jesus and his family lived. He and I studied Scripture together until he was a grown man, until he left Nazareth. They've all gone now. I miss them. An agreeable lot of people.

When Joseph died, Jesus was about eighteen or nineteen. He had been his father's right hand for some time, and took over as head of the family and bread winner. People liked him. He was practical and straightforward but no more ambitious than his father had been. As his brothers grew up, he taught them the skills of the trade as he had been taught by Joseph. Slowly, with patience. A born teacher. I once said that to him and he replied that he wanted his brothers to stay in the trade and know their craft because he had a feeling he would not always be a carpenter. Odd, that. For he did not say what he thought he would be – certainly not a preacher. His brother James, who came after Jesus, was the one with the preacher in him. Indeed, I hear that he is now very active in carrying on the work that Jesus began.

The family left here not long after Jesus left. They live in and around Capernaum. The two girls are married and I'm not sure where they live.

Mary is an interesting woman. Very quiet. A marvellous mother. One of those women born to be a mother. Very calm, very placid. A quiet voice. She ruled her brood with love, and no doubt still does. Judah, the youngest, was a very naughty boy, of violent temper, but she could calm him without raising her voice, almost without words. She has a quality of innocence, of being young. She has never lost the ability to be delighted, like a girl, by simple things. I miss her the most.

When we first heard about John the Baptizer here in Nazareth, Mary came in to see me. She told me that John could be related to her. She wasn't sure. She told me that just before Jesus was born she went to Jerusalem to visit an old couple who were cousins, or possibly her aunt and uncle, I can't remember. Her aunt, or cousin, told her that she, too, was pregnant and that the child was to be given to God to be brought up as a Nazarite, far away in the desert, to prepare him to do God's work. To 'prepare the way for one greater than he'. Mary said, 'So the Baptizer could be that baby. His parents died long ago.' She was quite excited. I said, 'It could be. Who is "the one greater than he", then?' The question had the strangest effect on her. She went very pale and I thought she was going to faint. I made her sit down. She was silent, looking into the distance as though she had just remembered something. Then she began to cry. She made no sound. She was like an unhappy child. Her eyes filled and the tears ran down.

Then Jesus walked in and went straight to her as if she'd called him. He knelt down and she rested her head against his shoulder like a tired little girl. He dried her eyes and they stood up. It is difficult to describe how they looked. Very still, very alone, separate. Apart, different, special in some way. Then Mary smiled and Jesus thanked me for looking after her and the moment passed.

It was only a few days after that, that Jesus told me he was going south to find John and be baptized. I was curious, for, since Joseph had died, Jesus had led the family in the same orthodox Jewishness always observed by Joseph. 'As a memorial,' he told me once, 'and because the religion is beautiful. My father loved beauty.' I was puzzled by this pleasant, hard-working carpenter's desire for baptism, which symbolizes cleansing, rebirth, repentance – none of which he seemed to need. I said so.

'You are an orthodox Jew,' I told him, 'and a good man. You do no one harm, and in your own way do a fair bit of good. You have a great knowledge and love of the Scriptures, for which I claim a modest credit, and you have an un-blemished reputation both as a man and a craftsman. It seems a needless journey.'

He said, 'I have no choice, my teacher. My love and know-ledge of the Scriptures indeed I owe to you. The meanings and prophecies I find in them are my own.'

It was oddly said. In no way abrupt, or rude. More as a statement of fact. I have thought about it often since his death. I think now that he meant that the prophecies and their meanings were about *him*, they were his *own*, it was *him* they meant. A frightening thought. The more so from a level-headed, well-read young man. Certainly he had great know-ledge of the words of the prophets. Often when we were discussing the inner meanings of this or that prophecy – a favourite intellectual exercise of mine – he would show sur-prise at my gropings and theories, and would say simply and with great certainty what was meant, especially by the pro-phecies telling of the coming of a Messiah. It was disturbing, for opinion upon such matters is usually offered only by our oldest sages – and then with hushed reverence, and tentatively.

I never checked him in this way of speaking, for usually there were just the two of us, and I did not mind. But, not long after he'd been baptized by John, he came back and preached in the synagogue here in much the same way. It gave great offence and nearly caused a riot. It was very ugly. The crowd threw him out of the synagogue and right out of the town. He never came back. I didn't blame him. In the middle of all the shouting that day in the synagogue he said, 'No man is special in the eyes of his family or neighbours.' It was quietly said, with some humour. Not many of us heard it.

I didn't see him again. Since he died, two years ago, I've heard a hundred stories about him. As a healer, as a miracle-worker, as a great preacher, as a prophet. Who knows what to believe? Perhaps his name will live on, who can tell?

SARAH

A large, fat, jolly woman, with a most infectious laugh, and a chuckling way of speaking. A great love for, and shrewdness about, people. Middle fifties.

When I first heard you were coming to see me, I thought you were a client – as my husband likes to call the people I work for – but I thought about it and I didn't see how you could be. People I find husbands or wives for don't just turn up, they are sent by people I know. Or they are relatives or friends of people I've arranged marriages for in the past. I suppose I'm the best-known matchmaker in this part of Galilee. Not just here in Nazareth, as far away as Nain and Cana! It's all recommendations, you know, I don't advertise. My husband says I'm good at making marriages because I'm nosey and a gossip and I know everybody's business. Well, maybe, but I *like* nearly everybody, too – and it's not that I'm so nosey (I am a bit), it's that people tell me things. Everybody talks to Sarah – and I listen more than I talk, believe me. I can be trusted, and people know it.

I'm not a clever woman, but I seem to be clever at putting people together. I don't think I've ever made a bad match. I'm not always successful, mind you. After all, *both* parties have to be willing. It's not only the girl's parents who come to me first, you know. Men are shyer than girls in most cases. Oh yes, positively. I won't deny I make a good living, but I don't do it only for the money. I get great happiness and satisfaction as well. I have ten thousand friends.

I was an only child and I know about loneliness. Sometimes I've seen someone and I've known at a glance that that person is lonely. Not sad, or unhappy – might be well known, have lots of friends – but I know that he or she is walking alone. What I call 'an apart person'. Now, to find a wife or husband for *that* person is a real happiness, a blessing from God – for God invented marrying.

Jesus was like that, you know. An apart person. Everybody liked him, and he was a friendly easy chap, with a nice voice and good manners. And good-looking, too. As things turned out, with him getting into so much terrible trouble and being executed, it would have been bad for any young woman I'd found for him. Great shame, he'd have made a good husband – and a wonderful father. You can take my word, I'm never wrong.

I'll be quite honest, I did try. About nine or ten years ago. He's been dead about a year and he left the town about three years before that, when he was about thirty. Yes, about nine years ago, when he was about twenty-four or -five. His father Joseph had been dead for some time and Jesus was head of the family and running a small joinery business with two of his brothers. I knew the family well, indeed Jesus did a number of jobs in this house. And I loved his mother, Mary, like a sister. I miss her very much, although I do see her from time to time. But it's not like her living round the corner, as she did for so many years. But she and the family were right to move away. Nazareth didn't deserve Jesus, who *was* a bi special. Still, it's over.

Well, as I say, I tried to find a nice wife for my carpenter. He wasn't a great catch really, a small-time woodworker of poor family. But he was hard-working and a good Jew. He knew his religion and observed it. And he was quite learned, too, you know.

Well, although Mary and her sons and daughters had exchanged many jokes with me, I'd done no business with them, as you might say. I always know when to stay away. But Jesus bothered me – and so did my middle daughter, Leah. Another apart person, another lone walker.

Now, I'm inclined to work by instinct. I trust my instinct – believe me, with good reason. But with Leah, who is precious to me, and with Jesus, I went slowly. I thought and thought. And I decided that I wanted him for my Leah. I wanted him in the family. He and Leah knew each other well. And that, you know, is the most difficult, to make old friends into sweethearts – and my Leah is no fool. She'd seen me at work too many times to be taken in by my little games. So I trod gently – a thing I'm not famous for – I went slowly. I found all sorts of woodwork that needed doing. I found lots of little messages for Leah to take round.

Well, I kept up this careful business for over two years and it didn't work. Although now, I think, Leah will love him till she dies. She is in Jerusalem with the Fellowship. When Jesus preached in the synagogue here, right at the start of his work, and the elders threw him out, Leah became his follower. One of the first. She came home and I knew at a glance she was in love. A shame, for I'd long given up hope. Oddly enough, and I've never told this to anyone before, my conviction that t was a lost cause as far as Jesus was concerned came from Mary. Truly. About two years *before* the synagogue business. You see, there's always a time when you bring the mothers together. A psychological moment, to talk in a different way.

Well, the mothers were Mary and me. And in five minutes knew she wasn't making the right noises. Very strange. Never before. I'll never forget it. She told me she loved Leah like her own, and that she could want nobody better for Jesus, but that it would be wrong and cruel to offer brief happiness and great sorrow to so fine a girl. I was speechless. Was Jesus ill with some terrible disease? Was he a bad man who would ill-treat my daughter? What could Mary mean?

Then Mary, who was weeping, looked up. She looked heartbroken.

'Don't ask me too much,' she said, 'I can't answer in any way that makes sense. But, before Jesus was born, and in the Great Temple at his circumcision, I was told things that meant that my splendid son, who gives me so much happiness, will one day give me sadness like a sword piercing my very soul. I feel it will all come true, and not long from now. I cannot help being "the woman of grief" in my son's life. I am his mother. You must protect Leah, my old friend, from such grief. She deserves better. Not a better man, there is no better, but a better life.'

Well, what could I do? Although, to be truthful, at that time they were not really closer than at any other time. There had always been a loving warmth. Jesus was a loving, warm person, like Mary. So I comforted Mary and told her there was nothing really to stop, it wasn't working anyway.

Odd how it's all come true. Leah will never marry, I don't think. But neither is she what Mary called 'a woman of grief'. She followed my carpenter to the end – and she saw that terrible end. Now she is with the Fellowship – and in her own way is one of the happiest people I know.

The Start of the Work

YURI

Rather plump, with dark, curly hair and black, lively eyes. Rather sunburned and healthy-looking. A strong, cheerful voice. Good clothes. Well-furnished home.

I was very sad when the news came that John the Baptist was dead. That was what we heard first; that he was dead. It was quite some time after, that we heard how he died, how he was murdered in the prison at Machaerus. Terrible business, but that Herodias was a terrible woman. Not that Salome is much better. What a thing for the Tetrarch to do – on his birthday, too. Although he's not a tetrarch now, of course. He's nothing; an exile in Gaul. Herod Antipas, banished by the Romans, by Caligula. I hope he never comes back. Over ten years since John died. Nine since Jesus. Antipas could have helped spare both, but he did nothing. A weakling; a fool. As the sons of strong men often are. His father, Herod, was not called 'the Great' for nothing.

John and Jesus. Marvellous characters, both. Neither of them was on the scene for very long but they certainly made their presence felt. I miss them both. How different they were – although I'm told they were related to each other. Jesus made you calm, and sort of happy. John frightened the life out of you! Do you know, I was there when they met for the first time? I will never forget it. It was not very far from here, where the Jordan meets the Salt Sea.

I made a sort of living out of John. He, right from the first, attracted huge crowds, and crowds get hungry, and food has been my family's business for generations. We grow it, we store it, we preserve it, we pickle it – and when John drew the crowds we would go out and *cook* it – on the spot! We are famous for it. Not that John ever sampled any of our goods. He never seemed to eat or drink anything. He was a Nazarite – and there's no harder way to live. Never to own anything, never to drink wine, or cut the hair or beard, endless prayer, to always be separate, alone, close to God. To drive yourself all the time. John lived in the desert, in the dry heat. He went barefoot, and wore a robe of woven camel hair and a heavy leather belt. The Scriptures say that Elijah dressed like that – and was a similar sort of man. Some say John was Elijah reborn. I don't know about such things. Food is my business.

John would stand on a little hillock or on a rock and the crowds would gather. Hundreds, from all over. He would stand still, waiting. He had strange eyes, which, until he began to speak would be without light, looking inwards almost. His voice was powerful, rather hoarse, full of energy – and doom! He gave little comfort. 'Repent!' he would roar. 'Change! Alter your ways! Wash away your sins!' Then he would lead the way to the river, or a stream, and walk in chest-high, and the people would line up and go to him and he would pray and duck their heads for a moment. People would come out of the water and dry themselves in the sun or go and change. They always looked happier.

Well, it was at the end of one of these days. A lot of the people had gone. John looked very tired. I was nearby, clearing up. One or two of John's followers were near him. Suddenly there was a sort of hush and I looked up. John was face to face with a man who seemed as relaxed as John was tense. They were of similar build. The man was of fairer complexion. 'I have come to be baptized,' he said. 'Do you want my name?' 'I know who you are,' said John, 'I have preached of your coming since I began to baptize. I preach and baptize people to prepare them for you. It's for them, not you.' John went on and on, almost refusing. But Jesus insisted, and a most beautiful moment took place. I saw it.

It doesn't seem like all those years ago. People sometimes

get cross with me – or jealous. 'You weren't there to be baptized,' they say. 'You weren't a follower, or disciple – of John *or* Jesus. You were a food-seller to the crowds! How come *you* were so close and saw so much?' Well, I wasn't a follower *then,* quite true. And I was close because a lot of the crowd had left and the Baptizer knew me. I fed his flocks. I cleared up after his flocks. He preached to them, and frightened them, and led them into the water and baptized them, and I sold them food and tidied up after them.

It was the end of the day. Late afternoon. The crowds had been huge. They usually were for John. He'd spoken in his usual doom-laden way, telling the people they must repent and change their lives; that they must *deserve* salvation. That being, as he put it, 'related to Abraham' carried no privileges. Powerful, sensible stuff. But also that day John had come back a number of times to the fact that he was only a 'messenger', to bring news of the coming of 'a great one'. 'I am nothing,' he shouted, in that hoarse, powerful voice, 'compared to him. I'm not fit to tie his shoe.' Many of the crowd that day were country folk, people of the land, and John used word-pictures they would understand. He always did; a marvellous man. 'The Great One will sort the chaff from the corn,' he told them. 'The chaff will be burnt. The rubbish on the threshing-floor will be cleaned away!' And so on. You must understand that at that time there was a great desire in people's hearts for a Messiah to come, a great hunger for a sort of new start. Everything had got so complicated; the simplicity had gone. The simple, great rules of Father Moses had become a vast rulebook that it seemed only the scribes and priests understood. John was simple. He made sense.

Anyway, as the sun was going down, there, suddenly, was Jesus. Asking to be baptized, in a simple, natural way. As I said, John was rather off balance. He didn't think it right. But Jesus insisted, and they went down to the river together. About fifty yards away. Some of John's followers went with them. I did, too. At the river bank John paused, but Jesus looked into his eyes and smiled and they walked into the water. The water looked lovely, catching the late sun. John didn't say much. Probably couldn't think of the right words in this special case. Understandable. When Jesus lowered his head beneath the water so did John. As the two dripping heads came up there was a change in the light. It was very odd. I looked up. We all did. Right across the sky, from the sun right across above us, there was a great band of light, as though we were looking up through an opening. Up into Heaven. Not a sunbeam; a gap. It was very quiet. No wind, no birdsong, no river noise, nothing. Then we saw, high up, a tiny, white, shining spot. It descended and became a bird, then, lower, a dove. A perfect beautiful dove. It flew down to Jesus and settled on his wet head. Then we heard a voice. A quiet, loving voice, like a father, which said, 'This is my beloved and only Son.' Now, whether I myself heard it, or whether only John heard it and told his followers and they told me, I'm not sure. It's a long time ago and a lot has happened. But I like to think I heard it, too.

SALOME

Mid-sixties. A cheerful, down-to-earth woman, looking younger than her years. Grey, abundant hair. Dark eyes of great liveliness. Solidly built, but not fat. A feeling of strength, and honesty.

Often I think how nice it would be if you could choose what your memory will hold. I've seen things I wish I could forget, and about other things I wish I could remember more. Ah, well!

You are not the first to ask me about when Jesus was a boy. I like to talk about him, he was my favourite nephew, it's no effort to remember. When he was a young man and his father, my brother-in-law Joseph, died, and he took over the business, I saw him less, and remember less. About his twenties I know little. He and his brothers were running the little joinery and my own sons were giving me grandchildren. From thirty onwards, till his death, he was very much part of our lives here in Capernaum. James and John, my sons, were among the first to follow him. People sometimes say 'Yes, well, they were his cousins,' as though that explains everything. It explains nothing. For a lot of it there is no explanation. Mind you, it is a sort of 'family' story.

John the Baptizer was a second or third cousin. His mother, my Aunt Elizabeth, God rest her sweet soul, was the first person that my sister confided in about Jesus. My sister Mary was always different from me. *I* was the one more likely to get pregnant before I was married! Mary didn't say a word to me when she knew she was going to have a baby – she went to old Aunt Elizabeth. I asked Mary why, not long ago. After all, I was her older sister, I was already married – and a mother! 'Why?' I said, 'why not tell *me*?' She always told me everything. She told me she was 'sent' to Aunt Liz. That, in any case, she didn't think I'd believe that no man was involved. She was right. It's only since Jesus has gone that Mary has told me and one or two others the story of the angel. Now; Mary is a sad, middle-aged woman. A widow, who watched her firstborn – and favourite – son executed like a thief. But she is as sane and level-headed as you and I. An angel, she says.

I don't think too deeply about it. Joseph married her well before Jesus came and it was a good marriage. He was a good man. Older than Mary, quite a lot older, but he was right for her. To this day Mary has a sort of 'young girl' quality, almost virginal. She adored our father. Maybe she found in Joseph a sort of another father. My husband, Zebedee, always said that Joseph was another Heli – our father.

As I say, I remember the early years more clearly than the later ones. Jesus would come and stay for weeks, either alone or with a friend – or one or two of his brothers. This has always been an open house, and it's always easy for a fisher-

man to feed his guests. And always work for them to help
with. The youngsters used to love going out on the boats.
They were perhaps the best years, when the boys were
becoming men. My two married in their twenties. Happy
times.

It was quite a surprise to me when one day James said he
was going south to hear John the Baptizer preach. It was an
even bigger surprise when he came back and told us he had
become a sort of disciple. I didn't take it too seriously. I asked
him what was so special about immersion in water. 'You spend
half your life immersed in water,' I told him, 'it's your living!'
He laughed. And next time he went to hear the Baptizer he
took his brother John.

Zebedee and I weren't too worried. They were both grown
men and they worked hard on the boats when they were here.
No harm. I think now that the Almighty was preparing us
for when they both decided to go with cousin Jesus. To go
with him, to be with him all the time.

It began in this room. Jesus was here on a visit and James
had just come back again from John the Baptizer. He was
full of it. Jesus listened to every word as though he'd been sort
of expecting to hear such things. He found out where the
next baptism meeting was to be and made a note of it. Not
long after that he and John met and John baptized him. And
it began.

You know, it was very difficult for me to see Jesus in a
different way. I'd known him all his life pretty well, he was
like a son. And then suddenly he was a preacher – and a
healer. He cured many round these parts. People I know. A
positive gift. Remarkable. A young carpenter from Nazareth.
And compared to my James and John, poor. They'd done
very well, my two. They and my husband were in partnership
with Jonas's sons, Andrew and Simon – although Jesus
changed Simon's name to Peter, and changed a great deal
else round here, too.

I'll be quite honest, I didn't like it. I've always been
ambitious for my sons. The family came first. My Zebedee,

bless him, was an energetic and well-liked man and he built a fair-sized business. We lived very comfortably, we lacked for nothing. We have another house in Jerusalem – where Mary now lives, with John and his family. Well, with his family more than John, who's hardly ever at home.

You see, it was so quick. One day the boys came round for supper and said that the Baptizer had called Jesus the 'waited-for Saviour' and, in no time at all, it seemed, Jesus was the most talked-about person in Israel. A marvellous speaker – and a man who seemingly could cure any disease or ailment. People would travel great distances – and wait for hours – just to see him, to hear him, to have him touch them and make him well again. Jesus, my favourite nephew, who used to help his Uncle Zeb to gut fish – and his Aunt Sal to cook them!

I must admit that, when James and John decided to leave the business to become full-time helpers of Jesus, I was against it. When they told me that Andrew and Simon were going to do the same, I thought they were all mad. Oddly, Zebedee accepted it. He somehow knew nothing would change what was to be.

I got very cross with Jesus once. He may not have meant to hurt Mary, but he did. I told him off about it. He hadn't been home to Nazareth for some months, and Mary was missing him. So she came here to Capernaum with her four other sons. They arrived in the evening, and Jesus was holding a big meeting, so I took them round to the hall where he was speaking. We went round to the back and I told them to wait while I went inside and told Jesus they were there.

The place was packed to the doors. He was by himself on a platform. I wrote a little message saying his family were outside waiting to greet him and had it passed to him. He took it, read it, and said to the audience: 'I am told that my family, my mother and brothers, are outside. Who are my family? Who are *really* my family? Anyone who does the will of God is my family. They are to me mother and brother and sister.'

Yes. Very clever point. But Mary heard it and was very hurt indeed. As I would have been, too. Needless and tactless. I told my miracle-working nephew exactly what I thought of him. He saw my point.

And yet you know, people are funny. I was just as insensitive to him once. Not long before he was executed. I think of it often and I always feel badly about it. Being ambitious for one's children is no excuse.

It was like this. One day James and John were home having a meal with their father and me, a rare thing. As often before, they were trying to explain to me what it was all about. Jesus's mission I mean, his campaign. The Kingdom of God and so on. Well, I got it into my mind that a sort of new order of things was to come on earth, with God's help, and that Jesus was to be in charge. The King. And all the miracles and healings and so on were to show people he was the right man for the post. Well, I thought, my boys were almost his first helpers, so they ought to get good jobs. I'll see to it, I thought, after all, I'm their mother.

So some time after this I heard that Jesus and the Twelve were going up to Jerusalem, and I decided that the time was right to go and talk to Jesus about the good jobs for my James and John. The time could not have been more wrong, but I wasn't to know.

I caught them up just outside Jericho, on the hill road. They were surprised to see me. They all looked rather serious.

Jesus greeted me and asked if he could help me in any way. I knelt down in front of him. I thought it right as he was soon to be a king. He looked rather startled. I said, rather formally, that I had come to ask a favour.

'What is it you want?' he said.

'When you are King,' I said, 'will you grant that these two sons of mine, your cousins and first followers, will sit on either side of you?'

Jesus helped me to my feet. James and John were as embarrassed and put out as the rest of the Twelve. They were all very cross and voices started to rise. Jesus stopped it, and, as often before, put it in simple terms. I think for my benefit. He explained that absolute power, in a heathen way, was not the idea at all. That the new kind of king, or leader, was not one who was served, but who served others. 'As I was telling you just before my aunt arrived,' he told them, 'soon I will be betrayed and condemned to death. I will be ridiculed and flogged and crucified. But through giving *my* life, many others will know a *better* life, will be set free. Thus *I* will serve *them*.'

Can you imagine how I felt? Could I have chosen a worse time to open my stupid mouth? Especially as it all came true.

JONAS

A large, handsome man, rather overweight and of florid colouring. About fifty-five. Greying hair and brown eyes. A humorous, amused expression. A warm, throaty voice, with expansive hand gestures.

When you sent me the message that you were going to pay me a visit so that we could talk about that wedding, I was rather surprised. For two reasons. Firstly, the wedding was quite some time ago. What is it, about six years? And secondly, I have very few visitors, let alone someone who comes a long way specially to see me and listen to me. My company and my conversation are not sought in this little town. Well, I can see their point. Here, in Cana, we have a town genius and a town idiot and a town ladies' man. I suppose I'm the town drunk. Not all the time, but often enough to support my reputation. Ah, well, never mind. Large villages or small towns are all alike, and Cana is no different. You'd think that the fact that the Carpenter was here twice and did magic both times would make a difference, but no.

The first time was at the wedding. I was told it was his first bit of magic anywhere. I was surprised to be asked to the wedding. I'm inclined to get a bit noisy in drink. Not quarrelsome or nasty; noisy. I sing and dance. Well, everybody should at a wedding. Anyway, I was there. The bridegroom was a nephew twice removed or something. The bride was related in some way to the Carpenter. His mother and brothers were there. She is a pleasant woman, Mary. Didn't really deserve all the trouble that came her way. Terrible thing to have a well-educated son put to death like a thief, with thieves. Terrible . . .

Where was I? Oh yes, the wedding. It was a fair-sized affair. The bride's father, whom I'd known a very long time, had done his daughter rather well. Tables inside and outside the house, a master of ceremonies, and plenty to eat and drink. Well, rather more to eat than to drink, I thought, but that I expected. He was worse than me when we were young but he married a strong-minded wife and she tidied him up. Maybe I should have married . . . although I don't know.

Anyway, it was a very happy affair. It was very nice to see Mary. I'd been quite friendly with her husband too, Joseph. He's been dead quite a long time. He was of Nazareth. I'm fond of Nazareth, although the people are a bit too strait-laced for me. I remember Mary was quite excited. She hadn't seen Jesus for some time. He'd gone south to see his kinsman, the Baptist, John. Another sad death, that one. Awful.

I'm not sure, but I think Jesus came late. I'm never sure about anything after I've been at a party for an hour or two. But I do remember quite clearly that he didn't arrive alone. He had, I believe, four others with him. Two brothers, who were fishermen, I remember, and Philip and Nathanael from Bethsaida, the other side of Capernaum. I knew *them* both quite well. I was surprised to see Nathanael with the Carpenter, for he had no opinion at all of anything or anyone from Nazareth! But they all seemed very close friends and very ready for a party. Which was a pity, because about five minutes before they arrived the wine had run out! The master of ceremonies was most embarrassed. So was our host, the bride's father. *He* deserved to be. I could hardly keep a straight face. I'd done my share but I wasn't the only one singing and dancing, I can tell you.

Well, I'm not sure exactly what did happen then. There was a sort of discussion between Mary and Jesus and his friends and a running to and fro by servants between the well and the great water jars on the porch. I was in the garden with the master of ceremonies, who was very put out. Very dignified man. An old friend. Then a servant came out with a goblet on a tray. My old friend tasted it and his face lit up. 'Is there more?' he said to the servant. 'Gallons and gallons!' said the servant. My old friend, as was his job, made a graceful speech to the guests pointing out that *this* host, contrary to custom, saved *his* best wine till last. He was right, it was a marvellous wine. Mary told me during the evening that Jesus made it. I told the Carpenter he was in the wrong trade. He thought it was a good joke.

AMOS

A heavily built man of about sixty-two or three. A feeling of wealth and authority. Well-spoken, with some humour. Large, well-shaped hands, used much in speech. A keen-eyed, alert look.

It's odd, I think, how hearing about someone or something after a long time sets the memory off. All sorts of connected details come to mind. In council this morning someone asked if there was any truth in the rumour that Pontius Pilate had committed suicide, that he couldn't get over his recall in disgrace to Rome and his banishment, and that he'd killed himself. I doubt it. I never liked him and I was pleased to see him go, the new chap is better, but, as I say, mention of Pilate – after, what is it, two years since he went? – sparked off all sorts of memories.

A trip I made to Nazareth came into my mind. With great clarity – and it's at least ten or eleven years ago. My wife

said she would like to visit her brother in Nazareth. I was
happy to agree. I had always had a sort of sentimental liking
for the place. My wife came from Nazareth and we had first
met there. I myself was born in Jerusalem, and, when we
were married, we made our home in the city. My work, both
as a merchant and as a councillor, made it necessary. My
work also kept me very busy, and opportunities to go visiting
family were few.

But it was the time of year when business was a bit slack
and I had a little time. So when she said, 'Amos, let's go
to Nazareth,' I said yes. Not that I liked her brother so much
– he was rather too strait-laced for me – but because our
visit was going to coincide with a visit to the town by this
young preacher that people were talking about. Jesus. All
sorts of stories were going round about him. How he'd turned
water into wine; how he healed people; and did miracles;
and was the Messiah – all sorts of stories.

One story I know was true – although it was some time
after our trip to Nazareth. He threw all the money changers
out of the Temple. Caused a great disturbance. It was dis-
cussed in council. A rather foolish action in many ways.
Temple dues and offerings had to be paid in the shekels of
Judea and people came from everywhere in the world to the
Great Temple. The money changers were necessary. Perhaps
some were a bit dishonest, but, nevertheless, a foolish action.

Not long after I'd first heard of Jesus, my interest in him
was increased by a fellow-councillor's rather odd reaction
to something I said. This fellow-councillor's name was Joseph,
an old friend of mine. He came from Arimathea, a pleasant
place near Jaffa – where Jonah caught the boat to Tarshish.
'Joseph,' I said, 'this Jesus is going to make a lot of enemies.'
'Maybe,' said Joseph, 'maybe. But I would give a great deal
to be his friend.' I was surprised. Joseph of Arimathea was
not young. He was rich and an orthodox Jew of good family.
A level, cultured, worldly man. 'He preaches like no one
else,' Joseph said, 'very simply. He teaches. He tells stories
to show a point. He gives off a sort of love.' So, when Joseph

told me that Jesus was going back to his home town of Nazareth to preach and my wife told me she wanted to see her brother, I made time. Joseph came, too.

Well, the young man did speak well – and caused nearly as big a disturbance as with the money changers! He spoke in the synagogue, on the Sabbath. He read from some of the prophecies of Isaiah and then made the lesson sound as though the prophecies referred to him! Caused quite a commotion. People knew him to be one of the local carpenters, a poor man. They said rude things. The young preacher took it well. 'No man is a prophet in his own town,' he said – and started to develop the point! The people got very angry indeed. They ran him out of town. I found the whole thing rather amusing. 'Still want to be his friend?' I said to Joseph. He was pale. 'More than ever,' he said, 'more than ever. I am a weak man and a coward. And to follow Jesus needs courage; the sort of courage I don't possess. But I will find a way to be his friend. I'll find a way.'

He did, too. And it took plenty of courage. I don't refer to his taking no part in the show of hands when Jesus was sentenced to death – a number of us abstained – but to his going to Pontius Pilate afterwards to ask for the body. Pilate was not only sick to death of the whole affair but he was also a very cruel man with great power. It would have been quite in character for him to have suggested that Joseph join his friend on the cross. Another thing that made the action brave was that the mob, although quieter after the crucifixion, was still unreliable, and could have taken Joseph's request to be proof that he was a disciple. A very dangerous thing to be on that day. All the disciples had gone into hiding. As I say, a brave man, Joseph.

Great Happenings

❖❖❖❖❖❖❖❖❖❖❖❖❖❖❖❖❖❖❖❖❖❖❖❖❖❖❖❖❖❖❖❖❖❖

REBEKAH

Late thirties. Rather plump. Fresh-complexioned, with dark hair and eyes. A relaxed and happy person. A clear voice of low pitch. An expressive face, in repose rather plain.

Simon, whom they now call Peter, is married to my younger sister. Andrew, his brother, is married to my second cousin, also younger than I am. I didn't think I would ever get married. But I am, and to the only man I ever loved, and I owe it all to the Carpenter. Jesus is dead, and gone. It's nearly four years since they killed him and I miss him as much now as I did when I first heard about it. I named my little boy Jesus.

My mother lives with me now. Seven years ago, when Jesus first came to Capernaum, I lived with her, in Simon's house. Not far from the synagogue and nearer to the shore, where the boats were kept. Andrew lived about four streets away. We lived well. Simon and Andrew and the sons of Zebedee made a good living as fishermen. They'd never done anything else. It's difficult to think of them now as preachers and healers. Jesus brought many changes to this family.

I've known my husband Yigal since we were children. We are much the same age.

When I was about sixteen and beginning to think about getting married, Yigal had his first attack. He tore his clothes and ran through the town screaming about death and devils. He frothed at the mouth and was like an animal. He did not harm anyone, although by the time he was cornered and locked up, he himself was scratched and bleeding.

The elders and doctors of the town examined him and then told my father that Yigal was possessed by a demon and that he would be kept locked up for a time. They said that marriage was out of the question, that the Laws of Moses forbade it, and that the Prince of Darkness would use the demon to father devil-children and crippled freaks, who would be blind or have extra limbs.

Yigal was kept locked up for nearly a year. He was calm and normal and remembered nothing of his attack. He was allowed out, and about a month later, when we were alone together in the little park near the jetty, it happened again. He went as white as a sheet and rigid in every limb. His eyes became huge and staring, seeing terrible things. Then he started to scream. I could do nothing with him at all. People came and he was put away again.

And so the years passed. My younger sister married Simon, and I prayed for Yigal. His attacks became more frequent, but, because he never harmed anyone but himself when he fell down or knocked into things, he was not locked away for more than a day or two. He would spend a lot of time in and around the synagogue sweeping and polishing and planting flowers. He knew every word of every service. People got used to him. He was harmless. The town loony, some people called him. Despite the fact that, when he was all right, he was as sane as – and better educated than – most of the people who called him names.

Then my father died, and my mother became ill. She used to feel faint and get a blinding headache and a terrible fever would begin. She would pour with sweat, and shiver. It would last sometimes for days, and would leave her weak and pale for a week or more. Simon was marvellous. He took us both into his house, so that my mother could have both her daughters near her when she was ill. It was practical and kindly. Poor Yigal would come occasionally for a meal, but he was poor company. Over the years he had become silent and frightened of his 'demon' as he called his illness.

Then one day Andrew started talking about the Baptizer,

John, who was preaching in the South. Andrew became a follower, and would go to hear John whenever he could. One day he took Simon, and they both came back talking about another person, a kinsman of John called Jesus, from Nazareth, not far from here. It seemed that John himself thought Jesus was very special in some way.

Well, about two months after that, Simon came in very excited and told us that this Jesus had decided to leave his home town of Nazareth and come and live here in Capernaum. My mother and I were a bit worried by the news, for Andrew and Simon – and the Zebedee boys, too, James and John – seemed to talk of nothing else but Jesus, whom hardly anyone had ever heard of. Simon told us that Jesus would arrive that night and stay with Andrew, and the next day, Sabbath, would speak in the synagogue. 'You come, too,' he said to my mother and myself. 'If you are there, Yigal will behave. You know how any sort of excitement sets him off.'

We said we would, but the next morning my poor mother began one of her bad turns, as bad as any she'd ever had. My sister stayed in to look after her and I went alone to the synagogue. Partly to keep an eye on Yigal but mainly to see this Jesus. The synagogue was packed. So was the women's section behind the lattice, which cut down how much I could see, except at the side, where there was a gap. But I was late and the space near the gap was crowded, and no one would move. So I heard more than I saw.

The service was normal up to the start where the rabbi or teacher speaks. Which was to be Jesus. He was the day's rabbi. He had a marvellous voice. Deep and strong, with a Galilean accent, which can be harsh, but in his case wasn't. He spoke simply, and seemed to have a sort of certainty, authority. We listened to it all and understood every word. He made word-pictures that we knew about, of fishermen, and boats, and catches, and working together, and mending nets, and being watchful of the clouds, to look upward often.

When he finished, there was absolute silence. Then Yigal began to scream at the top of his voice. It was absolutely unexpected, and frightened people out of their wits. Then I heard Jesus's voice cut into the screaming like a knife and cut it off. I fought my way through the crowd in the corner and looked through the gap. Yigal had fallen down and Jesus was helping him up. Yigal looked dazed but at peace, and happy. They walked out together, like friends. There was pandemonium. When I caught them up, Simon and Andrew were with them. I took Yigal's hand and he turned his head and looked at me. He looked different, the frightened look had gone. 'No more demons,' he said. 'Jesus said so. I'm cured.' And I knew it was true. I had no doubts at all.

I told Simon about my mother being so unwell, and he told Jesus. When we got home, we went straight through to her room. She was in a terrible state, shivering and flushed and burning hot. Soaked with perspiration.

Jesus stood near her bed and looked down at her. Her head stopped rolling from side to side and her eyes opened and looked into his. The shivering slowly stopped. A shudder went through her once or twice and then she was still. Jesus touched her hand. 'Come,' he said, and he and the men left. My mother got up immediately, and by the time my sister and I had helped her wash and change and do her hair, her high colour had gone and she was bossing us and worrying what to make for lunch.

The stories of my mother and Yigal spread like the wind, and, by the time the sun went down, there were hundreds of people outside the house. Sick people and their friends or families who'd brought them. Jesus put his hand on them one by one and made them better, even those with demons, like Yigal. The elders withdrew their objection and Yigal and I were married in the Spring. Jesus came to the wedding and he and the disciples (there were twelve by then) gave us a gift. It was a little demon, made of copper.

NOACH

About forty-two. Lean, strong-looking. In rough-weave robe and sandals. Uncut hair and beard. Lively, intelligent eyes. A friendly man, a warm, genuine smile, a deep voice.

You are not the first to ask me about the time that John the Baptist was in prison at Machaerus. Although it gives me some sadness to recall that time. I am content to do so — even glad — for it helps to keep fresh in my mind many remarkable things. It brings poor John back to life for me. Preaching, his face lifted to the sky, not locked away in Machaerus. Free, a voice. Not a silenced prisoner.

Machaerus. It was a strange place. More a fortress, or a fortified palace, than a prison. By itself. About five miles east of the Salt Sea, the Dead Sea. Enormously thick walls of the black rock common in that area. When Herod Antipas sent John there, six of us went with him. He was locked up. We, his followers, were not. We could come and go.

For John, one of the worst things about Machaerus was being shut away from the desert and the open air. He asked us for nothing; food and drink and comfort meant nothing to him.

'Go,' he would say to us, 'go everywhere. Bring me news of my kinsman Jesus. One of the things that sustains me in this place is the sureness in my mind that he was the one whose coming I was put on earth to announce. The Son of God. Bring me news.' And we would. But, as the time passed, we began to sense in John a doubt. He was no longer so sure in his mind. And one day he said to us, 'Go to Jesus and ask him plainly, for me, if he is the one. Or are we to look for someone else?'

We found Jesus up in the North, in Galilee, just ending one of his great healing meetings. We gave the message. He knew us. He told us to look around, to see for ourselves, to talk to people, and to go back and tell John of the cures, the spreading of God's word, the miracles of healing. 'Tell John,' he said, 'not to lose faith. Tell him his work goes on, his words live. His words were truth – and cannot be imprisoned. His words are free. Tell him I am the one.'

The two eldest of us went back right away to John. My cousin and I stayed behind. Huge crowds. Invalids and cripples and blind people. I spoke to John and James Zebedee, the first two followers of Jesus. We come from the same village in Galilee, we went to school together. They looked exhausted and dazed and spoke of the unbelievable and miraculous things they'd seen. 'Lepers have been cured,' John told me, 'people blind since birth have been made to see, the dead brought back to life.' Now, John and James were just ordinary fishermen. Rough, matter-of-fact men. Not men to be fooled, or easily taken in. I wandered about. I saw big Simon, now called Peter, and Andrew his brother. Matthew the tax-collector was there, looking much the same as before he decided to follow Jesus, but much more at peace. He was busy; they all were, all the disciples. They all seemed to have great skill in organizing the crowds. There was a sense of order, of peace. It is hard to describe.

I met that day Judas Iscariot. I didn't like him. Not a happy man. Hard, ambitious, but with a great belief in Jesus. For Judas, to be a friend of God's Son was important. John the Baptist was to him a fool for getting himself put in prison through being tactless. He said to me, 'If he'd watched his tongue, he could have been here today with us!' When I pointed out that Jesus wasn't too tactful either at times, he shouted, 'It's not the same!' and walked away.

Jesus did not think John a fool. Or anybody. Not even people who were. He finished the great meeting with a long speech all about John. A wonderful speech; it made me proud. 'A true prophet,' he called him, 'and far more than a prophet.' The huge crowd were silent, listening to every word. 'No one greater than John was ever born of man,' said Jesus. 'The man whose coming and purpose was foretold in the Scriptures. A messenger, a bringer of awaited news, a preparer of the way. The new way. Compared to great John,' Jesus told them, 'many people are like children who play in market-places at silly games. Children not old enough to recognize honesty and truth. John, who has lived all his life close to God in the most austere and self-disciplined way, is called by such people "crazy".' Then Jesus touched almost with humour on the dangers of him and his followers being 'normal', like everyone else, enjoying life. 'Then we are called gluttons! Who mix in bad company, who are *too* ordinary!' It was a wonderful speech. I wish John could have been there. The disciples were beaming. Not Judas. He was cross at Jesus for giving all the credit, as he put it, to the Baptist. I was never comfortable with Judas. Strange man.

My cousin and I moved on with Jesus and the disciples. We joined in, we helped, we saw astonishing things. When, a few weeks later, we arrived back at Machaerus, we were elated, full of news for John.

We were too late. Two days before, he had been beheaded, by order of Antipas – and his head passed round and shown to people as though it were a curiosity, a hunting trophy. I was told recently that Antipas has not slept well since; that, for a time, he believed that Jesus got his power from dead John; that, in the death of Jesus the year before last, he thought peace of mind would return. I was told that it has not. It seems just.

HESSETH

About sixty-two years old. Retired palace official, living now in a small villa on the shore of the Sea of Galilee. A quiet, rather sad-faced man, of slim build. Pale-complexioned, with grey eyes. A reader, and gardener.

If Antipas had not married his brother's wife, my son might

be alive today. Equally he might not. He was a soldier, and soldiers get killed in the course of their work. But, when Antipas decided to marry his brother's wife, he was married already. To a princess of Arabia – and a beautiful woman. He must have known that her father would see it as a terrible insult, as it was. And her father, King Aretas, took terrible revenge. He sent in an army and absolutely wiped out the army of Antipas, my son included. A bad time, a bad time. My wife will never get over it.

I've known Antipas since he was a boy. He was always jealous of his brother, Philip. Well, half-brother really. Different mothers. King Herod, their father, had ten wives. Vast 'inter-relating'. Not unusual in the great families. When Philip married Herodias, who caused all the trouble, in my opinion, he was marrying his *niece*. As a marriage, it seemed to work all right. They had a daughter, Salome, who, in her own way, was to cause nearly as much trouble as her mother.

When it was rumoured that Herodias was going to leave Philip and marry Antipas, I didn't believe it. I served the court all my life, and always in a personal-guard, close-to-the-throne, man-in-waiting sort of way. We knew everything.

But, apart from what seemed foolishness – and dangerous (as was proved when the army was destroyed) – it was also against Holy Law. Not that Antipas observed very much in the way of law, Holy or otherwise, but it was just not done to marry your brother's wife.

It is forbidden by God. It is written. As I say, I didn't believe it. I didn't believe that Antipas would make such a decision. I remember telling my wife, and her saying, 'Maybe Herodias made the decision that he would marry her. Women often do make up men's minds for them.' My wife was right.

A very strong-minded woman, Herodias. An immoral, cruel woman. But, in her own way, loyal. When Antipas went into exile some years ago, she went with him. An ambitious, hard woman. A good hater, as my wife would say. Certainly she hated John the Baptist. She never forgave him for de-nouncing her marriage to Antipas – and she arranged a dreadful death for him.

I met John. The day before he was killed. A very special sort of man I think. Quite fearless. Whilst the priests and the court whispered behind their hands about the marriage, he shouted how evil and wrong it was at the top of his voice. Everywhere. Until he was arrested.

They put him in the fort at Machaerus, by the Dead Sea, where only the desert hears a loud voice. I might never have met him, but once a year, on his birthday, Antipas used to move the whole court down to Machaerus for a few days, for a big celebration. A lot of guests, music, dancing, everything.

I did not think it was going to take place that year, because there were already rumours that the King of Arabia was massing his armies to wipe out the insult to his daughter, but the rumours were ignored by Antipas, who was quite besotted by his new wife. She dominated him, and everyone else, too. Frightening woman.

I was curious about John the Baptist. My son had heard him speak a number of times, and had become a sort of follower. Very little impressed my son, who was a regular soldier and a tall, powerful, outdoor sort of man. 'John makes you uncomfortable,' he used to say to me, 'stops you being self-satisfied, and too complacent.' I'd heard how thin and sunburned John was, how he dressed like a beggar-monk, how he had lived most of his life in the desert, in caves or tents.

When I met him he'd been in prison some time. Not so much in a cell or dungeon, as just locked up, to keep him quiet. It was in the afternoon. The King's apartments in the fort are far from the prison block. Machaerus is huge. I was taken down by a young warder. What I didn't expect was the stillness of John. And the remarkable eyes. They burned. They were more open than most people's, and you got the impression that they saw more. My son was right, he made you uncomfortable. I was aware of his own simple integrity, and, by comparison, the whole hill of rubbish in which I crawled. I remember thinking, as I sat down, that the choice of scented oil for my beard that morning had taken me twenty minutes. The curling of my beard by my servant, a half-hour.

I spoke to him about the birthday celebrations, and asked if he needed anything. He said he required nothing. He would not mention either Antipas or Herodias by name and had only contempt for them. Suddenly he asked me about Jesus, of Nazareth. 'My kinsman,' he said, 'a great man, a prophet sent by God. Jesus, whose birth and coming were foretold in the Scriptures.' I told him that I had heard of Jesus, that he was preaching regularly, that he was becoming well known, that he was said to be able to heal the sick and cure disease. He listened to me with his whole attention, without blinking. 'Then I am content,' he said.

The next evening was the great party. The biggest ever. Herodias had a great flair for such things. Every kind of rare food and drink, and between courses the most unusual and exotic entertainers. Drugs and aphrodisiacs were in the food and drink. The most sensual music was played, the heaviest incense perfume was burnt. 'There is no such thing as an orgy,' she used to say, 'only freedom. At my parties no one must wish, or desire, or want. Every wish and desire and want must be gratified.' She was decadence itself, a whore-mistress, a witch – for she knew men's minds. In the main, people, in her company, became as rotten as she was. She could bring out the worst.

Well, you know the story of how the night ended. Salome danced for the guests and Herodias told Antipas that the dance was his gift. She hinted that the dancer, her daughter, might also be his for a while. The company roared, although it was not a joke, and Antipas, who was more drunk and inflamed than his guests, told Salome she could have anything she desired. Then there was a silence, and the girl stood staring at her mother, who looked like a mad sorceress. The girl, I swear, was bewitched. She asked for the head of John. Then Herodias turned her eyes on Antipas and gestured that an officer swordsman should be sent to do it immediately.

Antipas, too drunk with wine and pride to retract, gave the order and the officer left. Some people started to sober up and wanted to leave, but Herodias forbade anyone to go. 'Not until my husband's order has been obeyed!' she screamed. 'Antipas, son of Herod the Great, must be obeyed!'

So we sat and waited. Then the main doors were flung open and the officer came in with four soldiers, marching. He carried in a shallow silver dish the severed head of the Baptist. The eyes were open. The officer strutted round showing the ghastly head to everyone.

People seemed to go mad; to become more crazed than before. They fainted, tore at their clothes, shouted obscenities, struck each other, screamed in fear, covered their eyes, rushed from the place like maddened animals.

John's body was buried by some of his followers. Soon the court moved back to Galilee and Machaerus wasn't mentioned any more. Herodias went on as before. There was a change in Antipas. A change hard to define. Some weeks later I was with him when some of his advisers were reading him reports about Jesus. 'A poor man,' they said, 'an artisan. A carpenter, of Nazareth. A healer, with positive cures, checked and proven. A preacher of some power, with a considerable following.'

Antipas sat silent till all had finished. They waited. Such careful attention was rare. Then he said, 'This Jesus must be John the Baptist. He has risen from the dead. That is why he has the power to work miracles.'

I've never forgotten the way he said it. With absolute certainty. Not long after this happened, the King of Arabia attacked. It was a massacre, and I lost my son. People say to this day that such a total defeat was because Antipas had killed the Baptist. Well, maybe. Doesn't make too much sense. Antipas is still alive and my only son is dead.

ITZHAK

*Tall, thin, about fifty-three. A pock-marked face with
many scars. A missing eyebrow adds to an already hard
expression. Thin, white hair, which like his clothes and
skin is spotlessly clean. A deep, hoarse voice.*

I was a leper. You needn't pull away, I'm not a leper any
more. I haven't been for some time. I'm 'clean', as the priests
put it. I've got a piece of paper from them to say that I have
been examined, that I have made the proper sacrifices, such
as I could afford, and that I have said the proper prayers
and all the paraphernalia with the lamb's blood and the oil
and the flour and the turtledoves has been carried out, and
that I'm clean. Not *un*clean, as before, but clean.

When the priests at last gave me the bit of paper, you'd
think it was they who'd cured me. I don't have a great deal
of time for priests. Not the Jerusalem lot. Leprosy is important. Not important enough for the authorities to provide
a little comfort for the lepers or a decent place for them to
live in – or die in. But if you get better, which can happen,
or get cured, as I was, it's straight up to head office for all
the performance and the bit of paper.

Don't think I'm ungrateful. I thank God every night. And
I say a prayer for the man who cured me. The Jerusalem lot
looked after him, too. They had him killed. I blame myself
a bit. I'm sort of famous. Everyone knows my story, certainly
in Galilee. I was one of the first cures that Jesus ever did.
Certainly the first leper. I often think to myself that I talked
him into it. Convinced him, gave him confidence.

He's been dead about a year, the Carpenter, and he worked
as a preacher and a healer for about three years before they
killed him. So I've been clean about four years. It seems less,
for I was unclean for a lot longer – about thirty years! I was
nearly twenty when I caught it. I'd been married about a

year and a half. My wife was pregnant. I was seen by the priests, who did all the examining and tests, as it says in Leviticus, and, when it was confirmed, I was sent away to the caves. My wife was passed as clean and, when the baby came, he was 'without blemish', as they say. She came from the North and I sent her back home. I divorced her and never saw the baby. It was best.

There are different kinds of leprosy. Some kill you quick. Others cripple you or make you blind. Another type covers you from head to toe and changes the face of a person with bumps and swellings. It's called lion-head, or, as we called it, 'the ugly'.

That was my kind. I'm not pretty now, but you should have seen me four years ago. Leviticus says you must live away from others, 'with torn clothes and bare head'. It says you must cry 'unclean, unclean' and wear a half-mask. The 'caves' where I lived served a large area of Galilee. We supported ourselves as best we could, and depended on charity. Lepers, in the main, just sit, or lie down. No energy, no strength. I was luckier than most, I was hideous but active, and I grew a little food and herbs. It was a simple life. You knew where you were. You were without hope. Simple. No problems. All in the same boat.

I heard about Jesus from a man who twice a week used to bring us some food. His daughter was one of us. He used to give us what news there was. We'd heard of John the Baptizer and his dipping people in water to make them pure again. A good joke that was, around the caves. We needed more than bloody water.

Anyway, this man told us that Jesus, who came from Nazareth, not far from us, and was a relative of the Baptizer, was getting a name for healing people. Not in Nazareth, his home town, they'd slung him out, but in other places. That bit sounded very genuine to me, so I listened carefully. This Jesus, the man said, had cured a woman of a high fever and made a man full of screaming devils sane again. With a touch, a word. For the woman's son-in-law, he'd arranged a miraculous great catch of fish.

On his next visit, the food man told us that Jesus was on a tour of synagogues, preaching every day, and that he was going to be quite near us, in a small town about four miles away, the next day.

I couldn't sleep, I couldn't rest. It was ridiculous, I'd long ago given up any hope. I was used to it, it was my way of life, a leper with 'the ugly'. But I couldn't rest.

The next morning I got up before anyone else and walked to the edge of the town. It was permitted, for begging purposes. And I waited. I didn't beg. I was never good at it, and if I went too close, my face, even with the bit of rag over half of it, was enough to frighten people to death. I waited till past noon. The sun was full on me, and I dozed off. I woke suddenly and about fifty yards away I saw him. Don't ask me how I knew. He was with other people and yet not with them. He was walking towards me and one or two were trying to stop him – for there was no mistaking what I was, mask or not. He put their hands away and walked on until he was no more than a yard or two away. I was riveted. No one ever came that close.

We looked at each other. His eyes were calm, and compassionate. He stood quite still. I thought he was weighing up the size of the job, so I helped him. I took off the mask. His expression didn't change, except – and I'm not sure about this – to look a little uncertain. A sort of power was coming from him.

I knelt down. 'Cure me,' I said. 'Make me clean.'

He said nothing. I was a bit dizzy in the hot sun. 'Try!' I said. 'Try! I don't ask to be whole again, or handsome! Just *clean!* Make a sign, ask God, say a prayer. *Try!*'

The tiny uncertainty was still in his face. I held out my arms to him. 'You can *do* it! You can make me clean!' I told him, 'You *can!* If you *want* to, you *can!*'

Then he smiled, as though remembering similar words he'd said to others. He came nearer and looked down into my eyes. Then he put his hand on my head.

'Certainly I want to,' he said. 'Be clean.' Then, very lightly, he passed his fingers over my face. I don't know how he could bear to do it.

Then his face became serious. 'Arrange as soon as you can to see the priests,' he said, 'your trial is over. By the time you go before the priests, your blood will be clean and clear of the disease. Your flesh will heal. You will pass all their tests, as written in Leviticus, and they will declare you clean. Make all the offerings and sacrifices laid down by the Law and God bless you.'

I was weeping. I couldn't speak. I felt no different and looked no different, yet I knew I was cured.

'One more thing,' he said, 'the most difficult. Don't tell anybody, not even the priests, how you were cured.'

And then he left me. All he said would happen, did. It took time, but I had no doubts at all. I didn't need to tell anyone, the story spread like wildfire. My cure, you must understand, was impossible. I was rotting away.

So I became a celebrity. A freak show. But I didn't mind. And, as the story was already known – and authenticated by the priests, bless 'em – I never stopped talking about the Carpenter. As things turned out, I may have done him harm. But I think he knew he was going to die young. I know about death. And I think he knew.

JOSEPH

Tall, rather bony man. Clean-shaven, rather long face, with vigorous grey hair and eyebrows. Steady grey eyes of some kindness. A feeling, however, of great strength and firmness. A deep voice. No hand gestures at all.

It is now about ten years since Jesus died on the cross. So many things have changed. I am glad that Pontius Pilate has gone. He was a cruel man who did not really like his job – or do it particularly well. People sometimes ask me why I didn't go back to tax-collecting after Jesus died. Well, there are a number of reasons, but one of them certainly was that I was happy to have no more dealings with Pilate and his tax department. Mighty Rome took heavy toll. It charged its subject nations high prices for being subject, and ruled, and occupied. The system they had once used was simple and direct – and open to much abuse. They would say, 'For such a district, so much,' and would sell to the highest bidder the collecting rights. As long as they got what they wanted, they would ask no questions about how much the collector had made for himself. Rome knew very well how greed can corrupt.

Over the years, the system was changed but the people's ignorance of how much they had to pay did not. Rome, and the Government, made few announcements, only demands. And the tax-collector, extortioner-turned-civil-servant, was the most hated man in the land. We were feared, and despised. We were welcome nowhere. We mixed with our own. We could not act on a jury, or be a witness, or be part of a congregation. We were sinners. We were called vultures and bloodsuckers and outcasts. But the job had to be done.

I worked for three collectors. The last one was Levi, or Matthew as he was known. He was an honest man – in that profession, a rare thing. He was rich, but you had to be. The treasury and Rome would not wait, but you might have to. Often the tax was a percentage of a man's crop; it could be wine or oil or wool or skins. So many taxes. Income tax; on certain articles a purchase tax; a vehicle tax. There were road tolls and harbour dues, and the markets were taxed. There were import and export duties.

People paid us unwillingly, as always. They lied and made excuses. They were tense and strained with us. Unnatural, full of hate. So you see, my friend, when Jesus came and stood in front of Matthew, quite relaxed, quite natural, steady-eyed, quiet, it stays in the mind. Matthew was not in a good mood, it had been a bad day. 'Name?' he said. 'District? Address? Goods or money? Occupation?' Jesus said nothing, and Matthew looked up. He recognized the Carpenter. So did I. We had been twice to hear him speak. He was well known as a healer. People believed him to be a miracle-worker. Not us. Tax-collectors as a class don't believe in miracles. We are shown the worst side of people and come to believe it to be the *only* side. We learn cynicism early.

Matthew and Jesus looked at each other without speaking, then Matthew got up. They were much the same in height, although Matthew was broader, older, much more richly dressed. A strong man. Well educated, powerful, realistic, hard-headed. He stood still, his eyes as steady as the Carpenter's. He seemed to be waiting. That morning he and I had been talking of how the sons of Zebedee, James and John, had given up their trade to join Jesus. We knew them. The story was that Jesus had just said, 'Follow me,' and they did. Without question. I waited; like Matthew. Then Jesus made a little gesture that seemed to say, 'This is a *life* for a man? This is to be *rich*?' Then he spoke. 'Follow me,' he said.

And Matthew did. He walked away from his tax-gathering table and never went back to it. No doubts, no hesitation, no looking back. I don't mean that he just got up and left his desk and his office and his staff just like that. He was a senior civil servant, an efficient man; and hard. He had to be. His mind was made up and it seemed that in no time he had arranged everything. Even a replacement for me; for I wanted to follow, too. If Jesus made sense to Matthew, that was good enough for me.

In a way, Matthew and I were close; he talked to me. I knew him well. I thought *very* well, but in the few days following his decision to give up his job, a new sort of Matthew emerged. Very calm but very cheerful. 'I'm going to give a big party,' he said, 'a sort of farewell party – or a start-a-new-life party!' I pointed out as gently as I could that, as tax-collectors, we were outcasts, pariahs, we had no friends; no one would come to the party. 'Pariahs will come!' said Matthew. 'Outcasts, tax-men like us, excise-men, customs-men, duty-collectors. A gathering of the hated, the feared, and the unpopular!' He roared with glee. 'And their wives and children!' Then he was quiet. 'The party will be for Jesus,' he said. 'Guest of honour. If he'll come.'

Of course he came. And with him came his first followers. 'My new workmates,' Matthew called them. The four fishermen, Simon-Peter and his brother Andrew, and John and James, sons of Zebedee. Philip came, and Bartholomew. They were all very different people. And Matthew was different again. I had the feeling that Jesus, village carpenter, chose very carefully.

It was a huge party. Wonderful food and drink – and music and songs. Jesus and his friends mixed easily and joined in everything. Jesus was very well known, a famous healer, a magnetic speaker. I was interested to see that at close quarters, in a noisy, crowded party, he had this same attraction. He spoke simply. You understood. If you spoke to him, he gave you his full attention; you were important.

During the evening, fairly late, when the party was at its height, a group of Pharisees and scribes turned up. These lovers of orthodoxy, these experts in the Laws of Moses, were the Carpenter's bitterest critics. They disapproved of him entirely. They came in, wouldn't sit down, wouldn't eat or drink, just criticized and were unpleasant. People were embarrassed and grew silent. Eventually everyone was listening, as they made their remarks and Jesus replied. He didn't get cross. He answered them with little comparisons and parables. He didn't call them inflexible or shut-minded or stiff or resistant to new ideas. He spoke gently of new wine that needs time to mature, of old garments too far gone to be patched. And, when they compared his followers with the fasting and praying disciples of John the Baptist and their own sects, Jesus paused. It was very quiet. He answered a little sadly; we did not know it was a prophecy. 'They are friends of a bridegroom,' he said. 'Should they not share the feast and joy of the wedding? But the day will come when their friend, the bridegroom, will be gone. *Then* they will fast and pray.' Matthew looked absolutely desolate. Peter, too. I will never forget it.

How well I recall that time. It seemed to me that the change in my life sharpened all my senses. And to make the change had seemed logical and easy – yet to be a 'follower' of someone or something was not really my nature. My brother was the 'devout', the 'believing' one of the family. He joined the Baptizer, John, when he first appeared. We called him 'The Disciple', my brother. I was the worldly one, the tax-man, with the good job in Matthew's office. Yet suddenly, here was I – also a disciple. Listening, being made to think in a new way, a more simple way. Belonging. I was happy and stimulated and proud.

Maybe proud in the wrong way, for, when the day came that Jesus chose his twelve whom he called 'apostles', I was not among them, and I was hurt, for I'd joined when Matthew did. I remember the occasion very well. There was a great crowd of us disciples and, surrounding us, an even greater crowd of people, of every kind. Many of them from far, far away. From all over Judea – from as far north as Tyre and Sidon. Many ill people, many cripples, many blind. We were waiting for Jesus. Tens of thousands of us. On the lower slope of a mountain, and on the plain below. Most of us had waited all night, waiting for Jesus to come down from the top of the mountain, where he'd gone to pray by himself. To be with God. We never disturbed him at these times – we waited.

We waited. We were quiet. It was cold, as always, before dawn. The huge crowd were quiet, too. A sense of something going to happen. Then the sky lightened and, as the sun rose and lit the top of the mountain, we saw Jesus. He came down slowly, thoughtfully, and the sun was on him all the way down. He joined us, and we crowded around. He greeted us with the easy friendliness that was very much his own, and then began to speak to us. To us, his disciples, not to the waiting crowds below on the lower levels of the slope. H said that there were to be twelve what he called apostles.

Matthew told me it was from a Greek word meaning someone who is sent out, an envoy, an ambassador. Then Jesus named the Twelve, and many, like me, were disappointed, although we all felt that Jesus, who knew men, had chosen the best. The last one named was Judas. Judas Iscariot, and as Jesus named him, he looked at him with a sort of sadness. He probably knew what Judas would one day do to him. Odd. I've only just remembered that sad look.

Then the Master walked on down the slope, and we all followed. The sun was now fully up, and it was warmer. The great crowds surged forward, bringing – as always – the sick and maimed to the front, for at that time the whole of Israel was talking about the cures and the healing done by Jesus. And that day he gave off his power like heat – you could feel it. Then he gave his great sermon – which people now call the Sermon on the Mount. Matthew was hypnotized by it – we all were. It seemed to turn every belief and law upside down and make even more sense than before. Matthew could quote the sermon word for word, and used it later in his own ministry. It was full of hope for the poor, the hungry, the sad, the outsiders. Full of love.

Matthew, as I told you, was a rich and sophisticated man – and before Jesus called him, a hard, cynical man. But not long after that sermon, I met him when he returned from one of his first trips as an apostle, and he was completely changed. Even his clothes. He looked like a poor preacher. He carried nothing. No staff, no purse of money, no food or water, nothing. 'As Jesus told us,' he said to me. 'He also told us that we would be able to heal the sick.' Matthew looked at me and smiled, a new, more gentle smile. 'And I can,' he said.

SAMUEL

Medium height, about sixty. A relaxed man, with a rather quizzical expression. Brown eyes. A large, handsome head. White-haired, but a feeling of vigour, energy. Deep-voiced, articulate.

I remember once asking my schoolteacher whether I had any chance of becoming like my father and grandfather. Absolutely orthodox and devout; obeying every religious rule, never forgetting anything. Fast or feast, prayer or blessing. 'Every chance,' he said, 'if your sense of humour doesn't get in the way!' I was slightly shocked, I remember. I thought he was being flippant. I'd asked a serious question; he'd given me a silly answer.

I told my mother, who laughed, and ruffled my hair and told me not to worry about it. As I grew older, I realized that my teacher had seen before I had that I would be rather like my laughing mother. She saw humour in everything, and it made her happy and popular till the day she died.

I also see humour, am also in my own way happy, although less popular. For the humour I have is an unerring nose for the ridiculous, the idiocy of men, the vanity, the hypocrisy, the whole mad comedy. So today, my father and grandfather safely buried, I am neither orthodox nor devout. I obey few rules, and fast rarely, I offer blessings to no one, and ask for none.

It was not always so. I was an only son and the disciplines of a very strict religious upbringing are hard. For generations my family have been watchdogs of the Law. Religious men, and men of religion. Not priests, but wardens; not spiritual leaders, but keepers of the rule-book. Inquisitors, men beyond reproach, heads of colleges. True Pharisees. Custodians of absolute conformity. Good men; sincere men. Men often in the middle of a forest unable to see the trees . . .

I followed in their footsteps, as expected. Sat in their seats. Took over their duties. Became grave, keeping the irreverent and humorous side of my nature, inherited from my beloved mother, firmly in check. If it all got too much, I would visit her and we would laugh till we cried. I miss her sorely.

A happening, when I was nearly forty, some twenty years ago, a happening sweet in the mind and beyond explanation, finally decided me to live in a way more agreeable to my true self. The self seen so clearly long ago by my teacher.

My mother's elder brother was born sickly, and, by the time he was a young man, had almost entirely lost the use of his legs. He had no belief in doctors at all, having been in their hands since birth. In the family he was known as Uncle Bethesda, which was not his name but where he spent most of his life. At the pools of Bethesda, here in Jerusalem. For years and years he lay on a low bed near to the Fifth Arch, by the smaller pool. He lay with other incurables, believing, as they did, that the first one into the pool 'after the Angel had moved the water' would be cured. An ancient legend. The trouble was that no one knew when the Angel would come – and there were many sufferers both nearer to the water and more active. So, for year after year, he lay there on his back, resigned, cheerful – he had my mother's humour – and pleasant. He was among friends; it was a community.

As I grew up, I used to visit him whenever I could – which was often. And when I left university and joined my father, I continued the habit. Later, when I took over certain religious duties at the Pharisaical College, my office was near the Sheep Gate, not far from the pools. It was no duty; I liked him. He was an interested, enthusiastic man, always encouraging, always proud of his nephew. When I was a little boy, my mother would leave me with him and the other invalids and cripples for hours.

Now, the happening. I was in synagogue one Sabbath. Passover time. The Pharisee Mother-Synagogue. Every part of the service perfect, as written, as laid down. To every side, the serious, stern, righteous faces. The service ended and we were filing out. Suddenly there was an excitement. One of the helpers at the pool came running. He was breathless, hardly able to speak. 'Quick!' he shouted, 'your uncle!' My first thought was that he was dead. I set off at once – it wasn't far – and some of the synagogue elders and my colleagues came too. It was good of them, but I would have preferred to be alone. Grief is a private thing.

As we drew near to the Sheep Gate we saw an amazing sight. Not what it was, *who* it was. As a sight it was ordinary. A man carrying a narrow bed on his head. Not unusual. A porter; a market carrier. Walking slowly, carefully. A man of about fifty-five, sixty.

It was my uncle. I stopped, my mouth open. I'd never seen him vertical. He saw me, and proceeded at the same pace, watching his feet walking, with a sort of wonder, smiling. He came to a standstill in front of me.

'A man did it,' he said to me, 'a young man. No more than thirty-five. Dressed poorly, with a Galilee accent. He stopped by me and we talked. He was friendly and had not heard the Angel legend. I was telling him how, when the water moved, I always missed it. How, in any case, I could never be first. "Do you really want to walk again?" he said to me. "Then get up! Walk! Get up, pick up your bed, and walk!" And I did. I had no doubts. I got up – I was very wobbly – and then I picked up my bed and I walked. And here I am.'

I felt strange. My uncle, always lying on his back, was part of the order of my life. I felt I was present at a great occasion; beyond my understanding; to do with God, and miracles. My uncle, with his bed on his head, stood smiling at me. Then the most venerable and respected of the elders stepped forward.

'Is it not written,' he said, 'that on the Sabbath it is wrong for a man to carry a burden? Do you not know it is wrong for you to be carrying that bed?'

The other elders lined themselves up by the one who'd just spoken. A jury; a line of silent reproach. My uncle carefully lowered his bed to the ground and looked along the line. Then he looked at me and started to laugh. He put his hands on my shoulders and laughed and laughed, like my mother, till the tears ran down. He hugged me to him, he hung on me, helpless, shaking, the laughter pouring from him like a great delirious wind of joy. Soon, for I put up no resistance, I was helpless as he, as wet with tears, as incapable of speech. The wind of his joy swept away for ever the dustiness of my life.

I picked up his bed and we walked away, not daring to look back at the line of motionless, affronted faces. Once round the corner, he stopped, drew himself up and straightened his features in a parody of the disapproval we had just left. He peered down at me, held it for a moment and then collapsed in hysterics. And so we made our way home, to my mother's, for Sabbath lunch. Two men, carrying an old bed, screaming with laughter, wet-eyed with joy and freedom.

GIDEON

Early sixties. A broad, muscular man, with heavy arms and hands. Rather bald, but with vigorous side-hair and beard. A humorous, weather-beaten face, with hazel eyes below big eyebrows. A deep, warm voice, with a rough, Galilee accent.

I have lived all my life here in Capernaum. It suits me. My family have been boatbuilders for generations, and it was my trade too. The lake, or, as some call it, the *Sea* of Galilee, gives a living to many people, certainly to folk who build and repair boats. I've never travelled much. Never been to Jerusalem, or Jericho, or Caesarea. Never seen the Salt Sea – or even the Great Sea, which is nearer. But plenty happens, or has happened over the years, in Capernaum, or nearby. More than people might think. It's not a big place, but it's a market town, a tax-collection centre – and a Roman military post. Plenty goes on.

I suppose what really put us on the map was Jesus. When they threw him out of Nazareth, where he was born, he came here to live. Good lesson; never try to impress your home town. I don't think he would have impressed *us* much (we were never short of preachers), but he began to perform those remarkable cures. You listen in a different way to a man like that.

I knew a number of the people he healed. One of the first, Peter's mother-in-law, was a distant relation of mine. Peter and Andrew and their father before them all used boats made in our yard. Boats take a fair time to build and your customers become your friends. I was at Peter's wedding. Great big fellow and tiny little wife. Lovely little person his wife is. Very capable, very level.

I remember very well when Peter and Andrew and the Zebedee sons joined the Carpenter. Very well. Though it must be nearly ten years. It caused quite a disturbance. Especially in old man Zebedee's life. Unbroken line of fishermen, the Zebedees, for God knows how many generations. Great place for gossip, a boat-yard, you get to hear everything. And I knew all the parties concerned in that first 'joining Jesus' – or the Carpenter, as we called him. I knew the tax-man, Levi – or Matthew, as he's known now. Well, everyone knew the tax-man. He was better than most of them. A hard man, obstinate and unbending. He changed a lot you know, after he gave up his job to follow the Carpenter.

Wonderful speaker the Carpenter was – and he had good, simple things to say – although some of his parables were difficult until he explained. But, as I say, it was the healing, the cures, the making people well again that first made him famous. One of these healings I was a bit involved in. Remarkable business altogether. Because the 'doctor', as it were, never met the patient. Never touched him, or laid eyes on him.

I knew the patient, although not very well. He was house servant to a friend of mine. An army officer. The Roman garrison in Capernaum numbered at that time about two hundred men. Two centuries, as they were called, under two officers, or centurions. My friend was one. He'd been in the town for a long time. A very well respected man indeed. Very good at getting people working together; very philanthropic. We have a fine synagogue in Capernaum that we owe almost entirely to his leadership and energy. And he wasn't a Jew. He was shifted to Cyprus about two years ago, just after Pilate was sent home. I miss him. Not Pilate, my friend. Nobody misses Pilate.

My friend, whose name was Caspius, and I became friends not long after he came to the town. We are much the same age. I learned a lot from him. He was a better-educated man than I – and interested in everything.

We spent a lot of time together. We went together to hear the Carpenter – when he gave his great speech up on the hill. What's called the Sermon on the Mount. My friend was deeply impressed; I thought it very dangerous stuff in parts. For Jesus, I mean. I was right as it turned out. Well, not long after this, Caspius told me his servant was very ill. 'He's been with me a long time,' he said, 'and I'm very fond of him. Nothing seems to do him any good. Do you think the Carpenter would help? Perhaps someone would speak for me.'

Typical remark. Not false modesty; *real* modesty. A rare man.

I went off right away. It wasn't difficult to find people to speak for Caspius. We went as a group and told Jesus about him. How he'd built a synagogue for the town. How fair he was in all his dealings. Jesus listened and said he would come immediately. I ran on ahead and told Caspius, who immediately – and very unexpectedly – became agitated. 'No!' he said. 'Go and tell him I didn't mean him to come *in person*, to go to any trouble. Just to give the order and that will do it. Tell him I know about orders. I'm a soldier, and I've taken orders and given orders all my life. I had to learn authority from men. He has it from God. Quick!' he said, 'go and stop him. Tell him just to give the order. It will be enough.' And he pushed me out of the house.

Jesus was just crossing the market place, now with a big crowd. I gave the message word for word. The Carpenter listened, then he turned to the crowd and repeated it. Then he said, 'I have never met faith like this anywhere.' He seemed full of wonder, and a sort of happiness. He walked back the way he had come and the crowd followed. I went back to Caspius with one or two others. We found him in his servant's room, helping him to get dressed. Although he needed no help. He was a bit pale, but perfectly well and lively. Rather apologetic about neglecting his duties. Caspius smiled and looked at us. He didn't look very surprised.

SHIM

Middle forties. A ruddy, open-air kind of man. Sturdy and muscular. Slow-speaking, like a man used to long silences or solitude. Steady, grey eyes. Big, capable hands.

You seem surprised to hear that I've never been across the lake, across the Sea of Galilee. Well, let me tell you that there are many people here in Gerasa who haven't even been out of the town gates. Why should they? How much you travel depends a lot upon what you do for a living, I think. A cousin of mine, who sells cloth, is *always* going across the lake – or round the top of it into Galilee.

Well, I look after pigs. A pigman, a swineherd. I've one or two of my own, but mainly I look after other people's. I've always done it. I know every inch of the country round here that's good for pigs. But not far afield, not far away. Pigs don't go far afield. And the buying and selling, the cattle market, is here in Gerasa.

It's a quiet place, Gerasa. Nothing much happens here, although your mentioning Jesus of Galilee brings back to me a remarkable day, remarkable. I don't often recall it, except with strangers. Most people here in the town remember it as clearly as I do. And, of course, it is some time ago now.

About ten or eleven years. Jesus has been gone, how long is it, eight, nine years?

Well, Jesus came here, to Gerasa, just once. And once was enough, believe me. I nearly lost my job because of Jesus – although I must admit that I saw remarkable things because of him, too. I know that since he died he has become very well known, but he wasn't then. He'd just started, and news travels slowly round here. At that time, too, the two sides of the lake were two separate provinces. We were Philip, Galilee was Antipas. If you count Decapolis, the ten towns, *three* provinces. Many changes since. They're all gone, Antipas, Philip, Pilate, too. And we are part of Syria. I don't change; I go on looking after pigs.

Yes, just once, Jesus came. By boat. He landed just south of the town, where the low cliffs are. I was up on top with the pigs. I saw this fishing boat with about six people in it and it looked as if they were intending to land at the bottom of the graveyard slope. Well, I left the pigs and started to make my way down to tell them not to, for it was dangerous, because of the madman.

He'd lived in the graveyard, in among the tombs and graves, for years, the madman. He was mainly the reason they closed it. People were afraid to go there. He was a tall, skinny man, filthy dirty, naked. His hair and beard were matted and crusty with blood, for he was always falling down and cutting his head on the stones. His eyes were ghastly, wide-staring open and sort of terrified. And he screamed from morning till night. Terrible noise.

I used to leave food for him. For weeks on end there would be only the two of us on that bit of shore, me up on the cliffs and him down among the tombs. I was used to him. If he came too near, I'd throw a stone and he would scream and run away and hide. I don't think he would have hurt me but I wasn't taking any chances. There'd been a time when the authorities used to catch him and chain him up, but then he'd go berserk, like a wild, trapped animal, and seem to have the strength of ten, and he'd break his chains and fetters and cover himself with cuts and bruises and blood. Pitiful.

So eventually they left him alone, poor soul. Left him to rot. A pigman's life is not much, but, when I used to see him, I used to count my blessings, and collect food for him. He became known as 'Shim's Friend'. People used to say to me, 'Shim, how's your friend?' and have a laugh. I didn't mind, if they put some food in the basket for my 'friend'.

But my 'friend' was mad, and full of demons and terror, and strong enough for ten, strong enough to kill anyone. So, when I saw the men in the boat, I started round the edge of the cliff, shouting. They didn't hear, and beached the boat. The madman was nowhere to be seen, so I decided to risk it and I ran down the slope through the graves towards the boat.

Jesus, although I didn't know it was him then, had landed and was walking up the beach. He waved his hand to me. I was about fifty yards away. Then, suddenly, half-way between us, the madman got to his feet from a clump of dwarf bushes. And began to scream. He had his back to me so I went on, picking up a big rock in case of trouble.

I heard Jesus say something, like a sharp order, a command, and the madman's scream took shape, became words, although I couldn't make them out. He seemed to be asking permission; there was fear in it. Then he was silent. Everything was silent. It was weird. The madman went to Jesus and sat down near him, looking up at him. There was no sound.

Then, suddenly, from the top of the low cliffs, the screaming began again tenfold. It frightened the life out of me. It was the pigs. I started up the slope to them. I thought maybe some wild dogs had got in among them. The screaming got louder and louder. As I reached the top, I was aware of a new noise. A great splashing and thudding. I stopped and looked round. Below me the graveyard sloped down to the Sea. To either side, the cliffs. And from the edge of the cliffs the pigs were jumping, screaming, into the Sea! Many, many more than my herd, hundreds more! Among them, pigmen from miles inland, shouting in despair and rage. It went on and on, and suddenly stopped. No more pigs. Silence. Down below, Jesus, with the naked madman sitting in front of him.

Well, the other pigmen and I rushed off to our farmers. We feared for our jobs. And what could we tell them? Only the truth – which sounded as though we were mad, or drunk! That some strangers had landed and done some magic and filled the pigs with mad demons which made them all jump into the Sea or smash themselves on the rocks below the cliffs! The word went round like a fire and half the town turned out, rushing back to the cliffs and down through the graveyard.

When we got back, the madman at first was not to be seen. Then I realized that the man nearest to Jesus was my 'friend'. Jesus and the fishermen had washed him and found some clothes for him, and there he sat, as calm and sane as I am. As I realized it and recognized my 'friend', so, it seemed, did everybody else. It was somehow more frightening than the pigs. The town elders stepped forward and asked Jesus to go away and not come back, as his magic was powerful – and very costly, for some two thousand pigs were missing. Most of the elders were our pig farmers, and I could see their point.

Jesus didn't argue. He and his friends turned and prepared to push their boat off. The madman went after them, imploring Jesus to take him also, but Jesus said no. Then, when the madman began to cry with gratitude, Jesus stopped him. 'God did it,' he said. 'God can do everything. Go and tell everyone what God has done for you.' And he and his friends sailed away.

Then there was an odd thing. The madman turned and looked up the slope at the people, then came across to me. 'Thank you for all the food,' he said. It came true about him being 'Shim's Friend'. He's more; he's my brother-in-law.

JUDITH

Middle forties. Dark hair and eyes. A gentle, smiling expression, an inner content. Slim, graceful, quietly dressed. The voice is low and pleasant.

This has been a special day in my life. Of a special sweetness, for my Deborah was married today, and of a special sadness, for the man who made her marriage possible was not with us to celebrate it. He has been dead nearly six years. He didn't deserve the death he suffered. To say that he rose again from the grave is of little comfort really, he is gone. His disciples are remarkable people, but they are not he. God's ways are strange indeed, if such a special young man had to suffer such a terrible death. Nearly six years, and it seems like yesterday. He should have been the Guest of Honour at my Deborah's wedding today. Instead, she and I talked a little of him, and, like women, wept a little.

How easily I say 'my' Deborah. She is related to me in no way (although she always called me Aunt). She is the only child of Jairus, who was the best friend of my late husband, David. They were two of the founders of the synagogue here. Deborah is part of my life. She was born about six months after my husband died. We were married only eight years and we were not blessed with children. Then David became ill and died and my life went dark. Not long after, I myself fell ill and began an internal bleeding, which took away my energy and my colour and my will to live.

Jairus and his wife, Anna, were wonderful to me. They are wonderful people. Anna had a difficult time when she had Deborah, and asked my help. It was just what I needed. To look after a family, to help tend a baby, to have a place, a reason for living. I suspect that Anna purposely stayed 'weak' for much longer than was true because she could see that her weakness was giving me strength – and joy. And what a lovely child my Deborah was.

I learnt to live with my complaint. When it was very bad, I would stay in bed and pray, and go as pale as the sheet, and try a new doctor or a new treatment. They were always bad times, depressing times, but always, too, there was Deborah to cheer me up. A golden-hearted child, a loving child.

The years passed. Deborah was nearly twelve and Anna and I began to plan a big party. We would talk for hours. It would be out of doors, with lanterns. A magician, a ventriloquist, puppets, Deborah's favourite dishes, which I would make.

It was during one of these talks that Anna first mentioned Jesus, 'A woodworker,' she said, 'from Galilee. A poor man, with a gift of healing.' She told me that he had cured a leper, a paralytic, a man's withered arm. He had taken the demons from people's heads and made them sane again. 'And for a widow, like you,' Anna told me, 'he did the greatest miracle. He brought her dead child back to life.'

Now, if you knew Anna, you'd know she is impressed by very little, least of all by magic-talk and hearsay. But she was serious and urgent. 'And he can cure you, too,' she said. 'It is said that if you yourself believe that he can, if you have faith, then he can, and does, in a minute.'

I couldn't sleep. I could think of nothing else. A few days later I heard that the Carpenter, as people called him, was coming here to our district, to hold a meeting. I had no more doubts. I was sure that God had sent him. I told Anna that I was going to the meeting and she said that she would also have liked to have gone but Deborah wasn't too well. Nothing serious.

I went to bed early, and next morning I was up at dawn, for the meeting was some way out of town, and great crowds were expected. I went by myself. I felt trembly and pale, but no more than usual. Someone let me ride a little way on their cart. Then I walked, and the crowds got thicker by the minute. I began to lose hope of getting near to him.

Then there was a great cry and people began to run and I was swept along. Someone took my hand and I looked up. It was Dov, a servant of Jairus. He shouted something about Deborah and let go and I lost him. I began to feel frightened, for I had little reserve of strength and the crowd was rough. I began to feel faint. I concentrated upon keeping my feet, I clutched at people, leaned on them. No one minded, I must have looked ghastly. The noise was deafening.

Suddenly, my part of the crowd slowed down. I pushed on, blindly. Then I fell to my knees. I was at the front. In front of me, a yard or two away, were more of the crowd, facing me, making a path. They were excited, looking to their left, pointing. I looked where they were looking and saw the Carpenter. I knew it was him, don't ask me how. Other men were with him – and by his side, Jairus. It was a surprise.

They moved towards me, the crowd pushing and jostling, closing in behind them. They drew level with me. I was afraid to look up. I was on my hands and knees. I prayed that the Carpenter would stop, and he did. His robe was brown and dusty. I reached forward and touched it. I knew with absolute certainty that touching his robe would be enough. It was. Then someone's knee caught me in the side and I fell over, hurting my elbow. But, as I fell, I knew that I was cured. A feeling of ease and strength came over me.

Jesus and his followers had moved a step or two and had again stopped. There was a sudden hush, for the crowd was more orderly just there, and it was not they who had stopped the Carpenter. He was very still, then he half turned. He was no more than four yards from me.

'Who touched me?' he said. He looked tired and pale. One of his followers, a big man, who I now know was Peter, said, 'Master, the crowds are huge, all around you, pushing and pressing. It could have been anyone.'

'No,' Jesus said, 'not that kind of touch, a touch of faith, in hope, for I felt the power go out of me.' He said it quietly. He looked drained. Then Jairus saw me and came over and

helped me to my feet. I took his hand from my arm and I
went to Jesus and knelt down and told him it was me. The
touch had been mine, in faith, in hope of a cure. I told him
I was now sure that I was cured, that the bleeding had
stopped and would never occur again.

'That is what cured you,' he said to me, 'your faith. Go in
peace.'

At that moment, Dov, the big servant of Jairus, pushed
through the crowd. People objected but he ignored them and
went to Jairus. I got up. I knew something was wrong.

'Master,' he said to Jairus, 'my mistress says that there is
now no need for the healer to come to Deborah. The child is
dead.'

I turned to poor Jairus. He stood like stone. I could not
believe it. The shock was tremendous, and, following the
shock, a feeling of great guilt. In a second I was convinced
that I had stolen Deborah's cure for myself. I began to
stammer and weep, hardly able to speak. Jairus, kind as
always, put his arms around me, told me that Deborah had
suddenly become very ill indeed, almost overnight, that she
had seemed unable to breathe, beyond help, dying. That his
going to the Carpenter had been desperate, the last hope.

'But I believed,' he said to me, 'I believed. I had faith,
like you, Judith. Perhaps not enough.'

Then Jesus spoke. 'Go on believing,' he said. 'Have faith.
Your daughter will be all right. Come!'

We went as fast as the crowds would allow, straight back
to Jairus's house. When we got there, the downstairs rooms
were full of noise. Jairus was wealthy, and every professional
mourner and wailer and dirge-player for miles around was
there, in full voice. The flutes and pipes and death gongs
were deafening.

'Stop the noise!' said Jesus. 'No one is dead here. The
child is asleep.' The beggars and wailers laughed at him.
Jesus told his friends to turn everybody out and they did.
Then he took big Peter, John and James, and Jairus showed
them up into Deborah's room, where I could hear Anna

weeping. I waited down below.

Then there was a silence. Not for long. Then they all came down. Deborah, too, her hand in the Carpenter's. Jairus was supporting Anna, who looked ready to faint. Her eyes were enormous.

'Are you Aunt Judy?' said Jesus. 'Well, Deborah says you know what her favourite dishes are. Make them. She's starving.'

I fed them all. Jesus told us to say nothing to anyone, but the whole town knew before we got up from the table. You can't keep such things quiet.

AARON

*About fifty-eight to sixty years old. Heavily built, mus-
cular, with full beard and thick eyebrows. A cheerful,
loud-voiced, likeable man. Well known locally for his
kindness and good humour.*

A woman-dominated man, me. Out-numbered and out-manœuvred. Mind you, I'm not complaining! Too late for complaints. And my girls, all four of 'em, bless 'em, are as good as gold. Two married (I've got seven grandchildren!) and one on the brink. The youngest, Rebecca, I don't think wants to get married. Still, you can never tell.

One of my sons-in-law is in business with me. We bake bread and smoke fish. As my father did before me. And where we work is perfect for it. Just above Tiberias. We supply all the northern districts, and with the fish an even wider area. Anybody can bake, I reckon, but smoking fish is something else. 'Out of the sea and into the smokehouse' is our motto, and it is fact. We are right on the shore, and the Sea of Galilee is full of fish, full. Also, just inland from us, a lot of the thornbush and hardwood grows that is best for the smoking. God is good.

You know, in this part of Israel the fishing is done by

families. Over the years we've traded with most of them. For a long time with the Zebedees, whose elder sons decided to follow their cousin, Jesus of Nazareth. For even longer with Jonas of Capernaum – whose sons Simon and Andrew did the same. Although I'm told Simon is called Peter now. Good fishermen, all of them. Nice families, nice people.

Andrew, you know, was first a follower of the Baptizer, John. A remarkable speaker, John was, remarkable. Strange-looking man. Lean as a twig, with hair which had never been cut and skin like sun-baked leather. A wild man. Yet no one ever laughed at him. Or, if they did, they stopped when he turned those eyes on them. Never seen eyes like it. I can't recall what colour they were, only the glow – especially in the brown face.

Jesus was a cousin of John, I'm told. Most of what I'm told I'm told by Rebecca, my youngest. Prophets and such are not my kind of thing at all. I know about baking and smoking. About loaves and fishes. But Rebecca knows more. She was there when John baptized Jesus – and when the four fishermen, whom she's known for years, decided to follow Jesus, she wasn't in the least surprised. She sort of did the same. She's no fool, my Rebecca. Hard-headed perhaps, obstinate – like her mother – but no fool. When she's in the bakehouse or working with the fish, she works as hard as a man. So, when she wanted a few days off to go on a trip with the Fellowship, as she called the followers of Jesus, I didn't object. A wandering preacher and his followers need looking after. It's best done by women.

Romantic figure, you know, Jesus. Pleasant, sympathetic sort of personality, a simple speaker – and a good voice. Warm and strong. And, of course, he came from these parts. One of us, sort of. And yet not one of us, somehow. This feeling he gave of being alone, by himself, apart, was perhaps the most fascinating thing about him. I miss him. Although I only met him once. The Zebedee boys brought him in once when they bought some loaves and fish. I heard him speak a number of times. Worth listening to. Most people aren't.

I always felt him to be a strong man. Not so much physically, although he was well made. He was a joiner-carpenter, and that makes muscles. No, I mean in character. He gave you the feeling that nothing would get him down, make him low in spirit.

But one day, and I was as close to him as I am to you, I saw that man very low in spirit indeed. And in circumstances which you'd think would have made any man happy. It was towards the end of one of these tours he used to do. He would speak and lead great prayer meetings and sick people would be brought to him and he would do these remarkable cures. Rebecca saw many.

Well, he was just outside here, on the jetty. All along the shore and spreading up into the streets, thousands of people. Nearest to Jesus, his closest followers, the Twelve, as they were called. Jesus looked tired, but at peace. Then Rebecca came in, very upset, with two young men who both looked as though they'd been on the road for days.

'They've killed the Baptist,' she said. 'They've killed John. They cut off his head.' I made her sit down, and the young men, who'd come all the way from the western shore of the Dead Sea, from the fort of Machaerus, told me the dreadful story of how that terrible wife of Antipas got her revenge on John for his criticizing her wicked ways. The young men, who were exhausted, told me that they had come to tell Jesus.

I sent one of my bakehouse boys, young Jonathan, to fetch Andrew. He came in and the young men told him the story. Andrew was shocked, and was silent for a while. Then he went out on to the jetty. I watched him go up to Jesus, and he did a gentle thing. He turned Jesus, so that they both faced out across the water, and then he told him.

The Carpenter was absolutely still for a moment, and then said something. Andrew came back with Peter and the Zebedee brothers.

'Jesus wants to get away by himself for a time,' they told me. 'We're going to sail him across the lake to Bethsaida. One of our boats is right outside. We are going now.' I told them to wait a moment, and I packed up five loaves and two freshly smoked fish for them. Even sad people get hungry.

And off they went. A lonely sight. Jesus by himself in the bows, and the others in the stern. No other boats anywhere.

The great crowd was puzzled, but the Fellowship went among them and explained. I expected the crowd to disperse and go home, but not at all! There was a sort of meeting and they decided to follow the Carpenter by walking along the shore round the top of the lake. At least ten miles. Rebecca, who'd recovered herself and had been out among them, came in with her eyes shining. 'See!' she said. 'See, people just want to *be* with him, to share his grief, to make it less. To help, as he helps us!' And off she went.

I didn't see her for two days. I wasn't worried. I pondered once or twice about how the great crowd had fared for food in Bethsaida, which doesn't much like strangers – and only has about three cafés.

Well, Rebecca told me that they didn't get as far as Bethsaida. When the crowd saw the boat, it was beached near a wide, grassy slope, at the top of which were some big rocks. The four disciples were by the boat and they said that Jesus was by himself in among the rocks, saying the prayers for the dead, for John. The great crowd gathered and waited. About five thousand, Rebecca said. It was late afternoon. Then Jesus appeared, and seemed deeply moved by the crowd's loyalty and sympathy. He moved among them, talking, smiling, laying on a hand here and there to heal someone, to cure someone.

I asked her what they did for food. After all, food is my business. I know the problems of large-scale catering.

'We all ate,' she told me, 'as much as we could eat. We were told to sit down in squares of about two hundred each. Which we did. I looked up the slope, I was sort of in the middle, and we looked like the beds in a kitchen garden. Down below, by the water, Jesus and the Twelve and a lot of the Fellowship men seemed busy breaking loaves and smoked fish into pieces and filling baskets they'd taken from the boats.

Then the baskets were brought up to the squares and we ate. There was enough for everybody. In fact there were twelve baskets-full left over.'

Now don't start asking me questions. I don't know how it was done. A lot of the people must have had food with them, because people on a journey always do have. A number of people bought bread and fish here before they set off. And pooling and sharing is one of the things Jesus taught. Rebecca keeps telling me not to look for too many answers. Not to question too much. She says that the God who can make the blind see and the paralysed walk can certainly do a bit of simple catering. Well, maybe, but making a few loaves and a couple of fishes go *too* far can be very bad for business. I told Rebecca that, in a joke, and she told Jesus. He laughed.

ELIAM

Old, thin, and weather-beaten. White hair and beard, uncut. Deep-set, grey eyes under strong eyebrows. A gentle expression. A slow, used-to-silence voice. A careful choice and use of words.

I am not sure how it was that Simon and I first became friends, although I must try to remember to call him Peter, as everyone else does these days, I'm told. I am told also that my fisherman friend seems to be engaged in large and rather dangerous work. I would say rather to his own surprise, for I know him well – and the spreading of the teachings of a dead preacher is not Simon's sort of thing at all. Not the Simon – or Peter – that I knew.

It is, of course, possible that he has changed. It is said that the Carpenter, Jesus, changed many of his followers, as, indeed, a special sort of man can. I never spoke to Jesus, or heard him preach. I saw him. Once. In remarkable, almost unbelievable, circumstances. Peter was there. It was almost the last time I saw my kindly and considerate fisherman.

As you see, I am not young. At least thirty years older than Peter, who must now be nearly forty. He was about thirty-three or four when Jesus died. They were much the same age. Yes, about forty Peter is now. I have known him most of his life, but not, as it were, to be 'friends'. He is like his father was, of the sea, of boats, of fish. I am of books, of words, of my first love, poetry.

So you see, my fisherman and I have little in common. Not even now, when he fishes for men, as he told me Jesus once put it. I do not fish for men, for 'readers of my writings'. I know few people. I live here on the side of the mountain, high up, alone, by choice. They tell me I am called the Hermit of Tabor. It's true enough.

Before I came here, to the mountain, I lived in Bethsaida, not very far from where Peter and his parents lived. I was very fond of his father, Jonas. A wise, quiet man. Peter's brother, Andrew, is very like Jonas, even to the voice and way of speaking. Peter was always the impetuous one, of great energy and strength. A vigorous, loyal man. The Carpenter chose his 'spreaders of the word' well.

I have always lived alone. I earned enough to keep myself by letter-writing for people, and by teaching children how to read and write, and to know their Scripture. I like children. I was a scribe and clerk to anyone who required such labours. Also, I had a certain skill in the drawing-up of a marriage settlement. On good paper, in pretty colours. I involved myself in no way with the arguments of the parties, only in their agreement – in pretty colours.

I think my friendship with Peter really began when he once brought a saying of Isaiah to me. He'd copied it down. He came in, big, handsome, not long married, in his middle twenties – and puzzled. He sensed a prophecy; about one who was to come as a 'Herald of the Messiah'.

Fishermen who think about such things are rare, and I was intrigued. We went into it. He got into the habit of dropping in, to talk, to tell me his news, to open his mind and his heart. He never came empty-handed. Fruit, vegetables, a chicken – and, most often, fish. I am fond of fish.

I remember his excitement when he first heard of the Preacher from the Desert, the Baptist, John. He was sure he was the Herald. He and Andrew made a trip south to see John, and to be baptized. It was on that occasion, or perhaps a similar occasion later, that he first met Jesus.

Not long after that, I moved away from Bethsaida, to live here on Tabor. This hut belonged to an old cousin of mine. He was dying; I looked after him till the end, and stayed on. Thus are 'hermits' made.

About two years later, at roughly the same time as I was considering a trip to Capernaum, where Peter and his family had moved to, Peter came to the mountain. Not to see me. A coincidence – and a fantastic happening for the Hermit of Tabor to witness.

I recognized him right away, and two of the three others with him. These were James and John, sons of Zebedee. They were his partners in business. The fourth man, a little ahead of them, was Jesus, although I didn't know it at that moment. Not for certain, but I assumed it was, I felt it was.

As you see, this hut is much overgrown by the two trees that hold it up. It is almost a tree itself. It is very difficult to find, for which I am grateful. I can see and not be seen. I was going out to greet the four men, but something about their silent ascent gave me pause. Jesus led, and the brothers and Peter followed, as though bidden.

They crossed the slope below here and then began to climb again, until they were about fifty yards above my two trees. They stopped and Jesus lifted his hand as though to say 'stay', and he walked up another ten yards or so. No speech; in fact, no sound, nothing. No birdsong, no wind, no tree noise, nothing. Then he began to glow. There is no other word. It was as though he grew white-hot. All colour went; he was pure white, the purest white, from head to toe. It hurt the eyes and I turned away. The three men, nearer to the brightness, had dropped, face down.

In the shade of the hut, behind eyelids closed and smarting,

I still saw the white figure. I turned again and opened my eyes. Now there were two more incandescent figures. One of great age and bearded, the other lean, in a coarse robe, leather-girdled. The three were speaking together, with Jesus listening more than speaking, as though receiving orders, or advice. With eyes nearly shut, I could just tolerate the brilliance of the light. Peter and the brothers lay still.

Peter raised his head first. In a second, he was on his feet, his voice thundering up the hillside. 'Moses!' he shouted, 'Elijah!' His voice was wild, hysterical, out of control. He shouted, out of wonder, in joy. I felt afraid.

Then the glow began to fade and the whole mountainside went into the shadow of a great cloud. I dropped to my knees and hid my head in my arms. Peter's voice died away and a voice a hundred times louder rang round the valley. 'This is my Son,' it said, 'my chosen. Listen to him!'

All was quiet then, and I got up and opened my eyes again. Jesus, by himself, natural, normal, was walking down to Peter. The brothers were on their feet. They listened as Jesus spoke quietly to them and then they all walked on down the mountain. They passed within twenty yards of my trees. I made no sound or sign. I felt weak and tired.

Living by one's self is conducive to visions, to fancies, to sounds in the head, to voices. I believe it happened. I believe I saw it. But when, about three months later, Peter made a journey to see me and I spoke of it, he denied it — after wanting to know every detail, as though for confirmation — and then said a strange thing. '*If* such a thing happened,' he said, 'such a wondrous thing, it is not yet the time to tell of it. There will come a time,' he said, 'when it *will* all be written down, *all* of it.'

'KWUZ'

*A nickname. Actual name not given. No age or origin.
About sixty to sixty-five. Bald, with an untidy beard.
Piercing, rather hard eyes in a permanently sun-darkened
face. A thin, rather cruel mouth, the whole expression
ungiving and watchful; sardonic. The voice rather loud,
and hoarse. Barrel-chested, with heavily muscled arms.
Poorly clad.*

Somebody once said, so I'm told, that Jerusalem has more
beggars than anywhere in the world. Whether it's true or not
I don't know, I've never been out of Jerusalem. And I've
been a beggar all my life. Certainly there are a great many
of us. We supply a demand. People *need* to be reminded how
lucky they are; to count their blessings. It makes them feel
good to give a coin. You'd think people with a lot of blessings
to be thankful for would give the most, wouldn't you? I
mean, it follows, doesn't it? Rich people, big givers. Like
hell. The givers are the poor people. Always have been.

As I say, as you can see, there's a lot of us. Local colour.
Good tourist attraction. Though I must admit, looking
around, a lot of us are not very pretty. We don't exactly
beautify the landscape. High Priest Caiaphas doesn't like
us cluttering up his beautiful Temple – and neither did King
Herod, who made it beautiful. We've been cleared out a number of times, but we creep back, you know, we creep back.
Herod's sons, Archelaus and Antipas, made similar noises. The
Roman governors, Pontius Pilate, all of them, tried to get rid
of us. We are still here. It's all a great game. Don't tell me
that most of us are perfectly able to do other work. I know. I'm
willing. What job would you suggest for someone with no
legs who can't read or write? I can manage without legs –
I've always had to – but once or twice I've wished I could
read.

One time in particular. I think of that occasion a lot. When Jesus of Galilee sat as near to me as you are. Just the once, I remember it like yesterday – and it's nearly eleven years. It's about nine or ten since he died. Nasty business. He was a remarkable man, the Carpenter, in many ways. I always felt a sort of kinship with him. We had things in common. No money, no possessions – and we weren't fooled by people. I know he loved 'em all and I hate 'em all, but we *knew* about them, they didn't fool us. I've sat on this stone seat, in this corner near the gate of this part of the Temple for nearly fifty years. I've seen it all. If I tell you that most people are not worth twopence, it's not because I've got no legs and I'm all twisted, it's because I've been observing people all my life. All day every day. I can't write a letter, or read a book, so I sit and watch the whole stupid comedy. The way people rush about and hurt each other and think they're clever. The way people seem to think that no one knows what they're up to. The beggars know it all.

We beggars have the most accurate and the fastest news grapevine in Israel. We know everything. I knew about the Carpenter being baptized by his cousin John the day after it happened. The wedding at Cana with the water-into-wine business, the loaves and fishes, the healing of the sick, the disturbance he made here in the Temple with the money changers, how they threw him out of the synagogue in Nazareth, everything. I could have told you the exact day that the authorities decided to put a stop to him. From that day he was a marked man. They were at every meeting, in every crowd. Experts in the Law, high priests, the 'Establishment'. But he could handle them. As I said, one day he sat here next to me. In the open. Talking to a huge crowd. Teaching, making it simple. Suddenly a gang of Pharisees and lawyers pushed their way through, dragging a woman. I knew her. A man had left his wife for her. Not unknown, such behaviour. Plenty of it went on. The Pharisees, a holier-than-thou lot, were there to make the Carpenter look a fool. Or to say something that they could hang a charge on. They pushed the woman forward and made a half-ring round her.

'An adulteress!' they screamed. 'Proven! Great Moses said such women must be stoned to death. What do *you* say?'

The crowd were silent. Some of them edged forward, looking for stones. Very little difference between a crowd and a mob, you know. The woman and Jesus looked at each other. Then the Carpenter sat forward and reached down and wrote something in the dust by his feet with his finger. His head down. He didn't hurry. The Pharisees and lawyers screamed for him to answer. He got up and it went very quiet. Then he said, 'Yes, she sinned. Let the first stone be thrown by the one among you who has never sinned.' Then he looked at the crowd, and they went as still as he was. After a moment or two he sat down again, very calm, and again he bent down and wrote with his finger in the dust. As near to me as you are. Very quiet.

Then people began to shuffle and the eldest of the party who'd brought the woman walked away. Then another. Then another. Soon she was by herself. Jesus lifted his head from the finger-writing and looked at the woman.

'All by yourself?' he said. 'Everybody gone? No stoning? No sentence? Did no one condemn you?'

'No one,' she said. She was crying. I wasn't surprised. Jesus got up and went to her.

'And I don't condemn you either,' he said. 'Go home and don't do it again.'

She went out by that gate, and the crowd moved forward to surround the Carpenter, to be near to him. Soon the writing in the dust was gone. And, because I can't read, I shall never know what it said.

RIVKA

About twenty-eight. Dark, good-looking, with a rather serious expression. Fine eyes. Slender and graceful. A direct, open way of speaking, with level gaze.

I suppose Martha and Mary told you where we live. They must trust you. That's good – although I hope they didn't give you the impression that Lazarus would speak to you. He won't, and I don't want him to anyway. Poor soul, it's best if he's not reminded too much of those times. The butcher told him last month that Governor Pilate has been recalled to Rome in disgrace and that was enough to stir it all up again for poor Lazarus. I'm not saying it's all nightmares and sadness for him, he can be as cheerful and loving as any other husband, but I do my best to leave certain doors closed. Believe me, I know best. He's out on the hills with our two kiddies and he's at peace. Talk to me. I know it all and I saw it all.

In one way Lazarus is right. The whole thing was full of echoes, of samenesses, of signs of things to come. When Lazarus gets in one of his states over it, it's mainly that aspect he's talking about.

It started with Martha's husband, Simon. He was a leper. He picked it up at the leper caves, where he used to take food and drink. He was a very good man. He was put away and in the first winter in the caves he caught some sort of lung fever and it killed him. About twelve years ago, just before Jesus first appeared.

Martha and Mary took me to one of the first faith healings Jesus did in this area. I don't know if you ever went to one. No? Well it's difficult to describe. It's not what you think. It was very quiet, for a start. Jesus was a calm sort of person. Unhurried. He never seemed to have any doubts about anything. He never doubted that he could heal – and he passed that feeling on, and the sick people believed too, and got better.

We saw remarkable things that day. When the meeting was over, Martha asked Jesus – who looked dead on his feet – and some of his followers, whom she knew, to come back for a meal, and they said yes. Now, mark this. Martha's house, 'Simon the Leper's House', is right at the end of the market street in Bethany. Beyond it, the path up to the top of the Mount of Olives, through the groves. As we came over the top and looked down at the house, Martha stopped and said to Jesus, 'If you had been here, Simon would not have died.'

Jesus looked at her without saying anything, then he kissed her and we went on down to supper. Martha as usual fussing and cooking and making everything just so, Mary just sitting and listening to Jesus.

Lazarus is the youngest of the three. He came about four years after Mary. He's never been very strong and I think his sisters spoiled him a bit. He and I are the same age. We grew up together. It didn't surprise anybody when we said we were going to get married. We set a date and started to get things together, and then Lazarus became ill. This was about two years after we'd met Jesus. He was a friend of the family.

People made jokes about Lazarus taking to his bed with 'marriage fear', but he got worse. He stopped eating and started terrible sweats and then after a few days went into a coma. The doctors were useless. Then Martha sent a message to Jesus, who was away to the east where the Jordan meets the Salt Sea. Fifteen, twenty miles. We thought he would come right away but he didn't. And Lazarus died. My father arranged the cave-grave with the rollstone in front and Martha and Mary prepared the body and put the bindings on. I helped. I insisted, and it is woman's work. Poor Lazarus. He was like wax. He'd given me a silk handkerchief about a month before and I bound it round his head. Then there were the prayers and the procession and he was put to rest in the cave and the stone rolled across. And still no Jesus. We couldn't understand it. Not a word – and my family is big, mostly living in Jerusalem, which is only about a half-hour's walk from Bethany. So every day there were dozens of people coming to sympathize or for prayers. But no Jesus.

I don't know how many days went by. Three or four. I just sat and cried. I was just nineteen. Then, on the Thursday I think it was, about midday, Martha came to me. 'Come,' she said, 'Jesus is coming.'

We met him at the top of the path where he had first kissed Martha. He kissed her again and she used nearly the same words as the first time. 'If only you'd been here,' she said, 'my brother would not have died.' Jesus didn't say much to us and then told Martha to fetch Mary. He and I stayed on the hill. Soon Martha came back with Mary and with them were a lot of friends and relatives who'd been in the house. Mary was in tears and so was everybody else. Then Mary sank down on her knees in front of Jesus and used the same words as Martha. 'If only you had been here, my brother would not have died.' Her voice was sure and her tears had stopped – and she's the emotional one.

By this time Jesus was in tears. It's very moving when a man cries. A lot of the people remarked on how much he must have loved Lazarus. Others spoke of his great cures, even the restoring of people seemingly dead or dying.

Then, as though by command, everyone turned and went down and across the hill to the grave. When we got there, everybody stood quiet. Jesus stood looking at the great stone with a strange expression. Frowning, thoughtful.

'Take away the stone,' he said.

'But he's been dead for days,' said Martha. 'By this time he will be decaying.'

'Take away the stone,' said Jesus, quite calm, like at one of his faith healings. 'If you believe, you will see the wonder of God.'

The men in the party rolled away the stone. The cave was a black hole. No one spoke.

Then Jesus looked up to Heaven and spoke in the same calm voice to God, calling him Father. Then he shouted in a tremendous voice like a great roar of trumpets:

'LAZARUS, COME FORTH!'

And Lazarus did. Not right away; after a moment or two. It was very natural and quite unfrightening. Rather endearing, in a way. A young man, very pale, rather sleepy, rubbing his eyes, blinking in the sun, with a silk handkerchief round his head.

Jesus looked at me. 'Take those clumsy grave-bindings off him,' he said, 'and take him home.'

Lazarus was perfectly well, and has never been ill since. Not in the body. We were married very soon after, on the date set. I've never known Lazarus so gay and happy. And then it seemed no time at all before the arrest, and the trial, and the terrible whipping, and the crucifixion, and we were standing in front of Jesus's grave, with the stone rolled back, and Lazarus started to talk about God giving and God taking away and echoes and samenesses and signs. I know all the stories about resurrection and so on, and of course Jesus, in the spirit, *does* live on, but Jesus, in the flesh, was *gone*. Lazarus is still here, and Jesus isn't, and Lazarus sort of blames himself. Poor Lazarus. He works very hard for the Fellowship, we both do, and he listens with sweet patience to everybody's wonderful stories of Jesus, but he'll never be happy again. It's worst late at night. He cries in my arms, like a child. 'Maybe Jesus was allowed just so many,' he says, 'and Lazarus was the last. Lazarus came back and Jesus didn't.' Poor Lazarus.

The Beginning of
the End

❖❖❖❖❖❖❖❖❖❖❖❖❖❖❖❖❖❖❖❖❖❖❖❖❖❖❖❖❖❖❖❖

BENJAMIN

Plump, rosy-cheeked, wide-eyed. Much younger in appearance than his twenty-five years. A gentle, high voice. A child-like innocence of manner. Left hand and foot slightly spastic.

For quite a long time, I thought my brother would get into trouble for letting the Carpenter and the Twelve eat their Passover supper upstairs. The way things turned out, I mean. With the Carpenter being arrested the same night and executed the next day. Sailing *very* close to the wind that was, I'd say. But my brother's like that, he's not afraid of anything. He's the strong one. He tells me what to do and I do it. He looks after me. He brought me up, pretty well, after my father died. He is nearly eight years older.

He's not really a follower of Jesus. He owed him a debt. Sharon, my brother's wife, was very ill. Dying in fact. No one could do anything, no one knew what it was. About two years ago, Jesus put his hand on her head and told her she would get well, and she did, in two days. My brother told Jesus that the big room upstairs was his whenever he wanted it – and for any purpose. For holding meetings, or for hiding in, when things got hot. My brother knows how things go in this city. In Jerusalem things can get hot – especially if you run foul of the Temple lot, or Governor Pilate. Jesus did both, I'm told. I only met Jesus once to talk to. On the night of that supper, upstairs. Nearly a year ago. It'll soon be Passover again. I like Passover, it's a happy feast, especially the Suppers of the First Nights, when the 'freedom from slavery' story is told.

The supper upstairs wasn't a very happy one. It was all rather strange. The whole day was odd. At breakfast my brother told me to clean the big room and put the long table up. I asked him who for, and were we going to have a Passover party. No, he said, the Carpenter and the Twelve were coming. I was surprised because Jesus had made no use of the room. 'When did you hear from him?' I said. 'Never mind,' said my brother. Sharon was pleased, and got busy cooking, getting all the big bowls out, making bread without salt, unleavened.

About midday, my brother told me to take a big water jug and go to the market well and fill it. *Very* odd. We have our own well in the garden. I was going to ask why but sometimes it's best not to. My brother usually has a good reason and the market is not far, and the melon-woman is by the well. I like melon.

I bought some melon and sat in the sun whilst I ate it. Then I picked up the jug and started back. And two men started to follow me! Both big, strong-looking men. It was obvious, they weren't secret about it. I tried to shake them off, I was a bit scared, but I couldn't. So I came home, so that my brother could handle it.

As I got to our door, they came right up and stood on either side of me, both looking down at me and smiling. The larger one put his hand on my shoulder. Then my brother opened the door and greeted them by name. Peter and John. It was two of the Twelve. Peter, the one with his hand on my shoulder, said he had a message from his Master, and we went inside. I took the water up to the room and, after a minute or two, they came up, with my brother, to see the room, and then they left.

I went on doing the room and helping Sharon with the cooking and in the late afternoon they all arrived together, just as the sun was going down, just as we'd finished the preparations. They stayed downstairs with us for a while and I

served them with wine and nuts and dates. Sharon came in
wearing her new Passover dress and they were nice to her
and the Carpenter asked her how she was keeping. She looked
very pretty.

They were a very assorted lot of men. About the only
thing they had in common was a Galilee accent. Except one,
a dark, rather tense-looking man called Judas who didn't
smile at all. My brother told me that Judas came from the
far south, from Kerioth; that his name, Iscariot, meant that.
Man of Kerioth. I didn't like him.

Some of the Twelve were cousins of the Carpenter. There
were two pairs of brothers, all fishermen. They were all rough
sort of men, even the one Sharon said had been a tax-collector.
She said one of them, who was quick and fiery, was a
Nationalist, anti-Roman, a revolutionary. There were two
called James, one a little, cheerful man. The biggest of the
Twelve was Peter. His brother Andrew was like him, but not
as tall or heavy. And he was quieter.

I suppose the quietest of them all that night was Jesus.
He listened more than he spoke, and seemed rather sad. Not
very Passoverish, as I call it, at all.

When I asked Sharon if she and my brother and I were
also going to eat upstairs in the big room, she said we had
not been invited. We were to have our own Passover supper
downstairs with some family, as usual, but I would help a
little upstairs with the serving and taking up of food and so on.

Then, when the sun had nearly gone, Jesus stood up. He
seemed rather tired. Everyone stopped talking and he led
the way upstairs. It seemed to be very solemn for Passover.

After a few minutes my brother told me to go up and
make certain they had enough water and towels for the hand-
washing before food. When I went in, it was feet that were
being washed! Jesus, the chief one, the head of them all, was
on his knees in front of Peter washing his feet and drying
them on a towel. He'd already done about half the Twelve.
There they sat, with clean feet. It was most odd – and all
rather serious. The Twelve seemed rather embarrassed. Ex-

cept Judas, who was scowling and looked angry. I went down and brought up more water and two fresh towels. When I offered to help, Jesus smiled and said no, and Judas gestured with his head for me to go out.

Our own supper, downstairs, was, as always on Passover, very happy, with lots of songs and wine. Every now and then I would go up to the big room with the large dishes of each course for them to serve themselves. They didn't seem to be enjoying themselves as much as we were downstairs. No songs at all. The second time I went up, they were just finishing the dish of savoury dip that Sharon always makes on Passover to start the meal. You dip bits of bread in, to give you a happy year.

As I walked in, about four of them were dipping and Jesus was saying, in a calm sort of way, 'One of you is going to betray me.' They all looked at him with their mouths open. I felt very out of place, and went out immediately. As I got to the bottom of the stairs, I heard the door to the room open and shut and then Judas came down. He was in a hurry, he nearly pushed me over – although I don't think he even saw me. He looked terrified – and sort of guilty. He rushed straight out into the street and up the road. I told my brother and he said it was none of our business and that I should take up a flask of our best wine with his compliments. I wasn't keen, and left it for a bit, then took it up when I took up the meat, the Passover Lamb.

I was almost afraid to open the door. When I did, the Carpenter was on his feet breaking pieces off a new loaf and passing them along to his friends. 'Eat,' he said. 'In memory of me; in memory of my body.' Then he saw me. 'And we will drink good wine,' he said, 'and it will also be in memory of me. Of my blood, which is soon to be shed for you.' I poured the wine in absolute silence. Jesus drank his and said 'I will drink no more until I drink it with you all in my Father's Kingdom.' I thought he meant his father was a king and he was a prince soon going home. He didn't look like a prince. As I went out, they were beginning a hymn, rather sad one. Not a Passover song at all.

The last time I went up was to ask if any more of anything was needed and to take up some of Sharon's cinnamon and almond cakes. I knocked but there seemed to be a lot of raised voices and I wasn't heard, so after a moment I went in.

Most of the Twelve were on their feet, all talking and protesting at once. The Carpenter was in the middle. Then he spoke, without raising his voice at all. 'It is written in the Scriptures,' he said. 'You will lose faith in me. All of you.'

The noise started again and the big man, Peter, spoke the loudest. 'Not me!' he said. 'Not me! Even if all the others do, not me!'

Then Jesus spoke again. 'I tell you, Peter,' he said, 'that before the cock crows tomorrow morning you will have denied you even know me – three times!'

The big man could hardly speak. I put down the little cakes and went downstairs. Not long after, they all came down. Jesus thanked my brother and Sharon and they all went out into the dark. They were all very quiet, not in the least like they'd been to a Passover party.

I went up to the big room and started to clear up. The little cakes were where I'd put them, untouched.

MALCHUS

About forty-five. Rather bald. A pale, bony face. Light hair and eyes. A sharp nose and a rather pursed mouth. A precise way of speech.

t would be as well, I would suggest, for you to understand ully that in the matter of the recent arrest and death of the Galilean I had no personal animosity toward him at all. None t all. And neither have my colleagues toward the ill-advised ollowers of Jesus, against whom they are at present drafting egulations. We carry out orders. We are servants of the Temple, with civil authority and influence. Civil servants, if

you like. We are bedrock; foundation. The leaders, the spokesmen, the ministers, change; governments change. We do not.
It was ever so; it will be always so.

Nothing personal. When my master, Caiaphas, said some
time ago that it would be better for Jesus to die than the
whole nation should suffer and be destroyed, he was speaking
good sense as he saw it. As a high priest he has a difficult
job – even with our help. Jesus is dead; the thing is done.
Soon he will be forgotten, but there was nothing personal.
When Caiaphas made that statement, I don't think he'd ever
met or seen Jesus. But miracle-workers and faith-healers and
raisers-from-the-dead can be very disruptive and troublesome
– and the Romans are touchy enough on the subject of what
my master calls matters religious. Pilate hates all religion, all
priests – high priests in particular. An impossible man, Pilate.

Certainly I have reason to be grateful to the late Jesus.
He attended to a head injury of mine that could have been
most disfiguring. I would like to have repaid him in some
way, but it was far too late in the day. Very apt statement
that, far too late in the day. And a fact. And what a day,
too. I would have liked to have spared him at least the
flogging, but that was by order of Pilate. A Roman touch;
crucify, but the scourge-whips first.

I'm told that the Galilean prophesied his death. So did I,
friend, so did I. I don't have prophetic powers, or second
sight. I have records. I have on record the exact day that one
of his closest friends, one of the so-called Twelve, came here
to give him to us. I say give; to sell him to us. It's always
a money transaction; it's allowed for. There's a fund. Cash;
unreceipted, in silver.

We took Jesus in a garden, at night. A detail of the Temple
Guard. Two officers, ten men, and the informer, to positively
identify. We knew that he would be with others and we
wanted no mistake. I went along really to see we got our
money's worth. Jesus, the leader. We were not interested in
the Twelve. Our experience in such matters is that, once the
ringleader is picked up, the 'followers' stop following and

fade away. We were right. They are all in hiding.

The big surprise was that one or two of them were armed.
Most unexpected. Could have been fatal in my case. When
the informer, Iscariot, had identified by touching, we went
forward to make formal arrest. At that moment one of the
Twelve, a huge, bearded man, stepped forward with a shortsword and very nearly took my ear off. I was covered in blood.
The blow had clubbed as well as cut me. I was dazed. I
heard the guard rush forward and a lot of shouting, and then
the Galilean's voice, speaking quietly. Someone put a bandage
round my head, almost holding the ear back in place. I
remember thinking to myself, 'Well, Jesus, if you're such a
healer, do *me*.'

It was almost as though he heard me. He put his two
hands up, over my two ears, and said, 'It will heal, there will
be no pain.'

He said other things, about prophecies coming true and
why were we so busy with guards, when we could have picked
him up in the Temple any time, and was he a bandit or
something. I paid little attention to him. I had no pain but
I hate the sight of blood and I was messy and sticky with it.
I left him to the men, who took him to the senior high priest,
Annas. Annas, my master's father-in-law. The Old Man, we
call him. The real power behind the throne, that one. He's
been high priest, *the* High Priest for years and years. He made
all five of his sons high priests, too – and when his daughter
married, his son-in-law, Caiaphas, as well.

Well, anyway, one of the soldiers took me back home to
the palace of Caiaphas and I went to my room and changed
my clothes and washed away the blood. I was going to change
the bandage, too, but didn't. Our reports said that Jesus had
positively cured people by the laying on of hands, and he'd
touched me. And certainly the pain had gone. I felt fine. I
looked down into the courtyard below my window. The palace
guard had made their usual bonfire. It looked cheerful. I saw
one of the arrest officers come through the gate on a horse
and I went down.

He told me that the Old Man would question Jesus and would send him across to us, to Caiaphas. The officer told me that he'd left as the interrogation began – and that the prisoner and escort would arrive in about two hours. I thanked him and invited him in for a drink. We talked, and he was surprised that my wound was giving me no pain, that I seemed unworried by it. He suggested that the garrison medical officer might look at it, perhaps put some stitches in. I refused. He didn't insist.

After a little while, one of the maid-servants came in and told us that one of the Twelve was in the courtyard warming himself at the fire. I asked her how she knew. She said she'd been to hear Jesus many times and the Twelve were always with him. She knew them all by sight.

'Is it the informer?' I asked her, 'Iscariot?'

She said no. I gathered she had no opinion of our informer. 'Are you sure?' I asked her. 'Did you speak to him?'

She said, 'Yes, I am sure. And I did speak to him. He denies it. He says he doesn't know Jesus.' She seemed upset. I sent her away.

I was amused. It seemed a foolish action on the fellow's part, whoever it was. I looked out of the window. There were quite a few people round the fire, many with their backs to me. I was curious, and I asked the officer to go down. I watched, and saw him speak to a rather big man for a minute or two and then leave him. He came in and went back to his chair. 'I think the girl is right,' he said. 'In fact, I think it's the man who hit you with the sword. He denies everything, and there's no blood on him. It was dark in the garden, and there was a lot of confusion, and I'm not sure. What do you want me to do?'

I looked down again at the man. He showed no signs of wanting to run away. He sat hunched, bulky, his back to me. I left it for a while until the officer said that he should go down to meet the arrest detail. I went with him.

The man had not moved. I went across to him. He stood up. He topped me by a head and a half. He looked down at me, at my bandaged head. I wasn't sure. I asked him his name, address and trade. Simon, he said, of Bethsaida, a fisherman.

'A Galilean,' I said, 'like Jesus of Nazareth, a troublemaker we now have under arrest. I think you are one of his gang. An armed bodyguard.'

He was looking across the top of my head. Jesus and the escort were just coming in. I kept my eyes on the big man's face. The good timing was not accidental; I know my job.

'Well?' I said.

'I don't know what you're talking about,' he said. 'I don't know Jesus.'

I turned and looked at Jesus. He was looking straight at the big man. A sad look, but nothing to prove he knew him. I turned back to the fisherman and saw an astonishing thing. Tears were pouring down his face. He tried to speak, twice, then he turned and ran like a madman across the yard and out of the gate.

I let him go. If he is one of the Twelve, and the movement, or party, or whatever it is, starts to get out of hand, we shall have him. I shan't charge him with bodily harm or offensive weapon. No point. The ear is as new. Perfect. No scar, nothing.

JANUS

Early fifties. Fit-looking, of a military bearing. Medium height, clean-shaven. Grey hair, cut close. A feeling of authority; also of tolerance, and humour.

Well, Pilate has gone. Cold-eyed Pontius, Procurator of Judea, rough-shod rider extraordinary, rode rough-shod just once too often and is on his way back to Rome. Good! Good riddance! Pilate, with pals in high places and appointed by Tiberius himself, is in disgrace and going back to a dying Tiberius, perhaps already dead – with new faces in the high places. Serves him right! Tiberius' favourite will be nobody's favourite, for that is the way of Rome.

I know Rome. I did my military service there and was born just outside, to the south. I came here, to Jerusalem, when Gratus was Governor, about fifteen years ago. He taught me my job. Personal assistant, aide-de-camp, right-hand man, dogsbody, beck-and-call merchant, doormat.

You must forgive me my rather undiplomatic use of words. Five days ago, when Pilate sailed away, I retired – and have not been quite sober since. The feeling of holiday is enormous. Marullus is the new man and he is bringing his own dogsbody. I shall see them in and that's it. I shall retire to my villa in Galilee, and my Galilean wife and my three sons, and I shall grow vegetables and fruit.

Where I was born we had a saying: 'You have to know a man really well to hate him.' Well, I knew Pilate very well indeed. He was by nature hateful. He had no friends, not really. Ten years here – and eight people saw him off. 'I like to leave a few reliable enemies wherever I go,' he used to say. He's left more than a few here.

He started off wrong. This country is really run by the religious groups – and he ran foul of them in no time at all. He used holy money, as they call the Temple treasury, to build waterworks, he ignored all the 'graven image' regulations here, he insulted people, he put the troops in at the drop of a handkerchief. The waterworks caused a riot and he killed rioters. He was a merciless man. Obstinate, and cold. Human life meant nothing to him. He once threatened me. I told him I was an army shortsword champion, and also that I kept a private journal to be forwarded to Rome upon my death. True, both statements. There's enough in that journal to hang him ten times over. He would execute without trial, condemn without evidence. He loved cruelty and pain for its own sake. He was corrupt and could be bought. He was crooked, but he was the law, Roman law, respected the world over. He was a bloody-handed disgrace. As you can hear, I knew him well enough to hate him. And I do. And believe me, I am not a good hater.

He was. He hated with a sneer, with contempt. He hated Antipas, and Caiaphas, the High Priest – and the High Priest's father-in-law, old Annas – who, I think, was a good match for him. An old fox, Annas. Completely unafraid of my splendid chief, he was. Pilate hated the Sanhedrin, the Pharisees, the Sadducees, all of them! 'I don't care what their labels are,' he'd say, 'they're *Jews*, the lot of 'em!' He had absolute contempt for Antipas – and *all* the royal family – and showed it! Not in a vulgar way. Never vulgar, my chief. A raised eyebrow, a curled lip, an expressionless look, like ice.

I suppose that one of the biggest disturbances in this last ten years was the business with the Carpenter, six or seven years ago. Not from Pilate's point of view, he didn't care one way or the other – and his killings were usually much bigger affairs, with him on his white horse and the troops in there with the swords.

No, when I say disturbance, I mean the whole city seemed to be in uproar. All the religious parties, the Temple lot, the councils, *everybody* seemed to be involved. Over a poor preacher from Galilee, who it seemed, could cure people. If Pilate had kept his temper and used a bit of sense, that preacher would have been put out of harm's way for a while and been forgotten. Instead of which, his followers have got a whole movement going which is right out of hand. We lock up ten and twenty more appear.

I often think that if the crowd with the preacher had waited till morning – and kept their voices down – we could have got some order into it. They came screaming into the forecourt at *dawn*! Hundreds of 'em! I swear that half of them were a paid mob. Shouters. We've used them ourselves. Confusion-makers.

Friend, I tell you that that was positively *not* the way to wake up my late chief – who used to indulge himself in various little ways till the early hours and normally opened the office at noon.

He came into my room white with temper. He looked mad. I dressed and went down, and the lunacy started. First, the accusers of the prisoner wouldn't come inside because we were a gentile-building and they didn't want to have their Passover holiness contaminated. So Pilate went out to them and told them to clear off and judge the fellow themselves. The shouters started then, wanting a death-sentence, which only Pilate could give. So he had the prisoner brought inside and questioned him.

The preacher either wouldn't answer, or answered in a way almost guaranteed to annoy Pilate. I was doing the charge notes. As far as I could make out, the preacher was accused of misrepresentation, fraud and blasphemy. He said he was King of the Jews and the Son of God. After a few minutes Pilate stopped asking questions. I think he could hardly believe that his sleep had been disturbed by the sort of case that usually was settled in a district court, with the prisoner given a week of cold-water immersion, starvation, and a straitjacket.

Pilate looked at me. I knew the look. It usually meant that some mad private joke was being invented. Jokes in which pain for others always played a part. Pain, ridicule, often death. That was his humour, his stimulant, his aphrodisiac. I do not joke.

And it began. First, out to the mob, and the listening, with inclined head and cold eyes, to the different party spokesmen. A tall, correct, sharp-nosed Pilate, saying, 'I see nothing criminal in the prisoner.' Then, when told the preacher was from Galilee, sending him over to Antipas, official Tetrarch of Galilee. Armed guard, all the trimmings. 'It won't wake Antipas up,' Pilate said to me. 'He's got his cronies in. One of his ghastly wife's three-day parties – with the "special entertainers". Well, here's a new one for them. A Son of God.'

When the preacher came back from Antipas, he was dressed in a gorgeous cloak. Obviously some pretty rough fun had been made of him. The mob went crazy, howling for death. Pilate was enjoying it. He made a speech about his custom of always releasing a prisoner at festival time. Anyone. Even the Carpenter. The shouters started to scream for a rioter called Barabbas, very popular in the city, to be set free, and for the preacher to be crucified. 'Are you sure?' Pilate kept on saying to them, 'Are you sure?' He got them screeching like children at a pantomime play. A Roman procurator, a governor. Disgraceful.

Then he told the crowd that, as crucifixion seemed rather too severe a punishment, he would give the prisoner a sharp lesson. 'He will be flogged,' he told them. 'Fifty strokes. With the Roman scourge-whip. Right away.'

The garrison yard is alongside the forecourt and the whipping could be heard. The mob counted the strokes. Pilate was watching them. He was absolutely relaxed, expressionless. He was sweating a little.

Two sergeants brought the preacher back. Still in the robe, with a ring of thorn twigs pushed down on his head. He looked half-dead. He couldn't stand up, he was held up. Twenty strokes is standard – and will take most of the skin off a man's back.

Pilate turned his head and raised a hand. 'Behold,' he said to the crowd, 'the King of the Jews.'

They screamed like wild animals when they've smelt blood. There was plenty to smell. They wanted a death, not a whipping.

Pilate got up and told the sergeants to bring the preacher inside again. 'For further interrogation', he said over his shoulder to the spokesmen. I think he was curious, as I was, to find out why what seemed to be a rather mild man should stir up so much riot.

He discovered little. The preacher was conscious, but obviously badly hurt. He was calm, and showed neither fear nor anger. Pilate asked him certain questions but he gave no reply at all. Just the calm, almost thoughtful, gaze. Pilate went closer. He was angry, a kind of cold anger, his own kind.

'Don't you realize,' he said, 'that whether you live or die is entirely in my hands?'

Then the preacher spoke. 'You have no power over me at all,' he said, 'except that allowed you by God, my Father. Indeed, in this matter, you are guilty of little. You do only as he tells you.'

It was said quietly, from a bruised mouth in a dead-white face. Pilate was speechless. I could see why. It was almost funny, unique. Here was a prisoner judging *him*, a prisoner flogged nearly to death, covered in blood, in a gory fancy dress of kingly robe and crown, assessing *his* guilt. And worse, here was the pawn in the game, the middle of the joke, seemingly the least disturbed – and the only one showing any sort of dignity.

Pilate said no more. To match the dignity, to show his own, he sent for the silver basin. The abstaining bowl. Warm water. We went out and the crowd went quiet; something new for them to see. I held the bowl, and Pilate, facing the priests, said in his formal voice: 'The charge is not proven, I wash my hands of this matter.' And dipped his fingers, with a sideways look at me.

Then it went bad. The old fox, old Annas, stepped forward. The mob, which had begun to go mad again, stopped.

'In this country,' said the old man, 'we have no kings any more. We have tetrarchs, and princes. And procurators, put here by our rulers, Rome. Who *do* have a king, an emperor. The accused says he is *our* king, enthroned by his Father, Almighty God. Thus greater even than the Emperor, than Caesar. If you release this man,' said the old fox, 'it would seem you agree. It would seem you are no friend of Caesar.'

It went dead quiet. Pilate was now the middle of the joke. It had blown up in his face. He had lost command, and the mob knew it. Mobs always know. And Pilate knew, as I did, that the old man had power, and could send a report to Rome, using that reasoning, that could make a *lot* of trouble. The hand-washing could be made to seem both incompetent *and* disloyal, both serious matters.

It was very quiet. The old man was absolutely unaffected by the hatred pouring out of Pilate, who tried to match the cunning of the old fox.

'Am I to kill your *King*?' he said to the old man.

'We have no king but Caesar,' said the old man, without blinking.

And that was it. Pilate walked across to the raised dais in the forecourt called the Pavement. He sat down on the small throne where judgements and sentences are given. He formally found the prisoner guilty and sentenced him to be crucified. He used the correct words, put his seal on the order, stood up, and walked past me without a word.

I didn't go to the crucifixion. If you've seen one, you've seen them all. The Carpenter wasn't the first, or the last.

LYDIA

Housewife. About thirty-eight years old. A rather buxom, good-looking woman. A ready smile, and a pleasant, low voice. The face, in repose, is serious and strong. Brown hair and eyes.

Pilate and his wife, my mistress, were in Israel about ten years and I can honestly say that I was as frightened of that man at the end as at the beginning. He was never cruel to me, or any of the house servants, but he did some terrible things. As Governor, or Procurator as he was called, he had absolute power. He killed many. He followed Gratus, whom we all liked better. Gratus used to talk about bringing more water to Jerusalem but did nothing. Pilate built an aqueduct – and took the money from the Temple treasury to pay for it – and put the city under martial law when it nearly caused a riot!

It was during that period I met my husband, Barabbas. He was well known in the city as an anti-Roman agitator. There was a whole bunch of them, and they caused a lot of trouble.

They were called Zealots. All sorts of people called themselves Zealots, from the roughest gutter-boy to highly educated scribes. Even lawyers, and priests. My Barabbas, bless him, was nearer gutter-boy than priest. He's quieter now, but when he was younger, before Jesus was crucified, he was a terror. And very handsome and popular with the ladies – and he knew it! I disapproved of him entirely. I come of what is called a respectable family. We've been in service to the royals or the Roman governors for generations. I was a lady's maid, first to the wife of Gratus, and then, when Pilate came, to *his* wife. I miss her very much indeed. A lovely person, Lady Claudia.

Barabbas and I are both followers of Jesus. They shouldn't have killed him. He did no harm. But killing him made him live, if you know what I mean. Oddly enough, I first heard of Jesus from Barabbas. On my days off I used to go to a social club in the West End of the city. I liked it, it was lively. A lot of servants of the palace and Government House and so on used to go. It was well run. It was there I met Barabbas, as I said, just after the aqueduct disturbances. He and his friends had been trying to stir up the unrest into a full-size war against the Romans. Very naughty, very silly. When things quietened down he and some of the other younger Zealots used to come to the club. Very earnest lot, most of them. Lot of students among them, wanting to change the world. Fat chance, it was a Roman world.

Well, I was telling Barabbas about Pilate's wife, my mistress, and her bad dreams and nightmares. She used to suffer terribly. She would wake screaming and rigid – or for days she would be afraid to sleep, and would get pale and exhausted, poor soul. Pitiful to see. And she hated taking stuff. Any sort of drug upset her. So I told Barabbas and he told me about this preacher, Jesus of Nazareth, who it seemed could cure people of anything. Leprosy, blindness, fits, anything.

I told my mistress and she went to one of Jesus's meetings. I went with her. She didn't get near enough to speak to Jesus there was a great crush of people, but on his way out of those meetings he used to walk slowly, and the crowd used to keep running forward to form lines either side of him, and we did the same, and as he passed us he looked straight into my mistress's eyes. She didn't say anything and neither did he, but that same night she began to sleep better. I can't explain it. She believed; and it was enough.

I was grateful to Barabbas and I let him take me out a few times. Away from his wild friends he was very nice – and he respected me, too. A bit too much, I thought, for he had a wicked reputation as a lover, and I wouldn't have minded. But not once did he try to take liberties or go too far. He would have been the first. After we were married, he told me he knew that – and he wanted it kept that way, until he married me! Very sure of himself he was! Less so after Jesus died.

If Jesus hadn't died, I wouldn't have my Barabbas. Although it's about ten years ago now (Pilate's been gone nearly four years), it's well remembered how the mob screamed for Barabbas to be freed from prison and for Jesus to be killed. It could have been the other way round. Pilate had this rule of releasing one prisoner on every major feast day. Barabbas and two of his friends had been caught red-handed in some sabotage nonsense, and they'd stolen some arms from the Roman garrison. It was all very brave and stupid and dangerous and they were put in prison and became sort of heroes. They were sentenced to death, but Pilate set no date. He was waiting for things to calm down. Then, not long after, Jesus was arrested.

I remember every detail of the morning Jesus was questioned by Pilate, who was in a foul temper. Any sort of delegation or council or committee brought out the worst in him, and that morning it seemed that every elder and high priest and lawyer in Jerusalem was screaming and shouting at him. Pilate shut them up and made their spokesmen make the charges. Then he began to question Jesus, who hardly answered him, which made him angrier still.

I heard about that part later, because I had my own troubles. My mistress, who'd been sleeping normally for months, woke that morning screaming and terrified – worse than before she went to Jesus. She was in a dreadful state. I had to slap her and throw cold water in her face to bring her round, to wake her up properly. She babbled and wept, and when she'd quietened down she asked what all the shouting was outside. When I told her it had to do with Jesus, she jumped up, with staring eyes like a madwoman. 'Go to Pilate,' she screamed at me. 'Tell him to have nothing to do with this matter. Nothing to do with Jesus, that good, good man. I have had such dreams, such terrible dreams – of death and massacre and disgrace and banishment and blood and exile! Tell him to have nothing to *do* with it! *Nothing!* Go and tell him!' she screamed, '*tell* him!'

Well, I did as she asked, I went to the forecourt and told Pilate. He listened without changing his expression, his eyes as cold as ice. Then he turned to the great mob and asked them whom they wanted released, Jesus or Barabbas. They roared for Barabbas – and that Jesus should be crucified.

Which was done. Barabbas and I were at the crucifixion. How could we not be? It changed Barabbas. Me, too. We married soon after. Some people blamed Barabbas, which was stupid, it had nothing to do with him.

Six years after Jesus was killed, my mistress's dream came true, sort of – although she never told me the details of the dream. Pilate heard about a great crowd of harmless treasure hunters in Samaria and he sent in an armed force and killed hundreds. Death and massacre and blood. The Samaritans complained to Rome and Pilate and his wife were recalled to Rome and then banished to southern France. Disgrace and banishment. I heard he committed suicide. I doubt it. My poor mistress. She changed, also, you know, after Jesus died. She was a follower, too, in her own way. She helped the Fellowship a lot, on the quiet. And she never had another nightmare.

SYLVANUS
(A second visit. See page 31)

I think I may have told you, at our first meeting, that Great
Herod liked continuity in his court. He trusted no one, but
liked the faces of those he didn't trust to be familiar.

It was often said at court that it was better to be a servant
of Herod than a relative of Herod. You would live longer.
It is an over-simplification, but not without some truth.

I served Herod till he died; then, in the sharing-out between
the sons, Archelaus – till Rome got rid of him – and then
Antipas, until Rome got rid of *him*, about two years ago.
Antipas the Tetrarch, part-ruler – for after Great Herod,
Rome wanted no more kings. And after Archelaus, even the
tetrarchs would have Romans to show them the way it was
to be done. Roman governors, procurators.

When Antipas was officially made Tetrarch of Galilee,
some months after his father died, it was one thing. After
ten years, when Archelaus was sent away, it was another. The
governors came. Coponius, Marcus Ambivius, Annius Rufus
– during whose time Great Augustus died – then Gratus, of
whom I was fond, and after him Pontius Pilate, of whom I
was not. When Pilate came, Antipas had been a part-ruler,
a tetrarch, some thirty years. Procurators had been in the
country for twenty. I knew them all. They were in some ways
alike; bred for the job. A sort of regulation-book courtesy,
but with a certain hardness.

Pontius Pilate was the fifth – and the hardest. He took one
look at Antipas and saw him for the weak, woman-dominated
fool he was. I think they had met in Rome, where Antipas
met Herodias – who did the dominating, but neither ever
mentioned it to me, and, in a limited way, they both confided
in me. I was an old employee, a sort of family retainer, privy
councillor, and senior civil servant rolled into one. I did not
mind. It appealed to my sense of humour to be a go-between.
Antipas has gone now, in disgrace, but he was no fool.

Foolish, yes, and weak, but he was able – and had inherited his father's love of creating fine buildings, even cities. Tiberias he built, and a lot of Sepphoris. I knew him so well. Pilate, less well. But the Roman was an enclosed, shut in, frightening man. He, too, is gone now. He went before Antipas, also in disgrace.

Such different men. In every way. Certainly in the matter of their private, off-duty, lives. Pilate was no angel, but compared to the occasional goings-on among the Antipas family and friends, he was ascetic. When Herodias, that dreadful woman, made Antipas kill John the Baptist, she did it at a *party*, a wild party. At which her stupid daughter, Salome, danced like a whore and her weakling of a husband had a good man killed so as not to lose face. Pilate was full of contempt. He had met John, as I had, and rather respected that fearless, wild man. As I did.

Not long after the Baptist was beheaded, we began to hear of another preacher. A man of Galilee, from Nazareth, Jesus, son of Joseph. Over a period of two or three years, he became quite famous. The orthodox and conservative groups didn't like him at all and finally arrested him. At night.

The morning following that night comes often into my thoughts – although it must be nearly ten years ago. There was a happening that morning that brought together Pilate and Antipas (whom he'd always detested) in a sort of closeness they had never shared. They became almost friends from that morning onwards. Very strange. I remember it well – and the happening – with a particular distaste.

It was Spring time, Passover time. Antipas and the court were in Jerusalem, as usual, for Passover. I had come with them from Galilee and seen them in, and had taken a few days off, to come here, to my own house.

It was a Friday, quite early. The sun was only just up. I was asleep. There was a loud knocking on my door. My servant came to me rather alarmed. It was a two-soldier escort, to take me to Pilate. As soon as possible. To do with the matter of the arrested preacher, Jesus. I did not know he'd been arrested.

When we arrived at the praetorium, the forecourt, the parade yard was full of people. Hundreds. Screaming, shouting, hurling accusations at the man I took to be Jesus, up on the steps, who was silent and still.

The soldiers went through the mob like a knife through butter, very roughly indeed. Pilate waited for me on the terrace at the top of the steps. He took me into an anteroom. He looked very angry. I assumed, quite rightly, that he had been awakened in much the same way as I had, but even earlier. Also, he was rather a stickler for correct procedure in the matter of judicial examination, and the mob outside were near to riot. I said so.

'And being whipped up, too,' said Pilate. 'I know the signs. Paid agitators, professional troublemakers. It's all out of hand. The preacher doesn't matter – there are too many of them anyway – but the charges against him are very minor by law. Obstruction, unlawful assembly and so on. I think he's some sort of religious maniac. The Temple lot are in a lather about him. Seems he says he's the King of the Jews and the Son of their God. Lot of rubbish. But I've just been told that he is from Galilee, which, strictly, is under the jurisdiction of Antipas. So I'm passing this little lot over to him. Let *him* handle it!'

Well, off we went, across town, to the palace. Antipas, as usual, had a crowd of guests. Parties at the palace were three-four-day affairs. Everyone was up – or hadn't yet been to bed.

A rubbishy lot. I knew them all. All looking a bit jaded. For Antipas, Jesus and the yelling crowd and the high priests and lawyers were just the thing the party needed. He'd never met Jesus, so he set him up on a throne.

'If he says he's King of the Jews,' he giggled to his guests, 'let's treat him like a king!' He had Jesus dressed in a gorgeous robe and he and his ridiculous friends danced and pranced and bowed and laughed themselves sick. Then Antipas, full of half-drunk self-importance, asked questions of Jesus, demanded 'proof', used long words. 'Do *me* a miracle,' he said. 'Raise somebody from the dead for *me*! I'll kill somebody! You provide the magic, I'll provide the corpse! What would you like, male or female? I can arrange it in a minute. Young or old? With a head or without?' He roared with laughter, and then stopped. John the Baptist had been a relative of Jesus.

To all this nonsense Jesus answered not one word. He sat quiet. Then the palace guard of Antipas had *their* fun – and the lawyers went on shouting. Every kind of charge.

I watched Antipas. He was very ill at ease. Herodias spoke to him and laughed – and he shouted in her face. Most un-usual. I didn't hear what he said. She moved away, very drunk. He pushed his way through the crowd to me. 'Take the fool back to Pilate,' he said. 'I don't want anything to do with him. He bores me. Get him out of here. Get rid of him. Immediately!'

I asked him, because I could not resist doing so (and also I objected to his tone), whether he wanted the robe back. 'It is a royal garment,' I said, with a little mischief, 'and the preacher says he is a king. It might appear to Pilate that you in some way agree.'

He started to shout at the top of his voice. Half-mad, dis-connected gibberish.

We took the preacher back to Pilate. He was crucified that afternoon. Pilate did not care one way or the other. He had no regard for human life at all. He had enormous power, and great cruelty. To scourge before execution was barbarous – and the preacher was not the first – or the last. I do not miss Pilate.

Although I do not think that Pilate would ever admit it, that morning he bowed to the mob. The Temple lot hinted at trouble if he didn't – and he did as he was told. It was to his interest, it suited his book.

As I said, from then on he and Antipas became quite friendly. He probably found that in the matter of weakness he and Antipas had a lot in common.

ALEXANDER

About fifty. Tall, heavily built, with big shoulders and a handsome head. Black hair and eyes. Dark skin. A musical, deep voice. Friendly, warm.

When I look back, it seems to me that the whole thing had a sort of pattern, a shape. I'm not a superstitious man, or particularly deep-thinking, but I'm not young either, and age gives a sort of perspective. Paul of Tarsus said that to me a year or two ago and he is no fool. Indeed Paul's own life has had a pattern and a shape that no one could have foreseen. He and I had been talking of my father. He knows my father very well, and loves him. Most people do. He's old, my father, but he's a bit special. And in his own way he's rather famous, even now, after nearly twenty years. Simon, who carried the cross for Jesus. My father, when he is sad, or thinking back, makes a little joke: 'The heaviest work I ever did,' he says, 'and I didn't get a penny for it.'

My brother Rufus and I were born in Cyrenaica, in this city, Cyrene. My father's family has been here for generations. Fruit farmers, as we are; as my father was. A perfect place for fruit, Cyrene. About two thousand feet above sea level, with the sea, the Great Sea, only five miles to the north. And a fine city. My father always says that of the five cities, the Pentapolis, Cyrene is the finest. Only one other place in the whole world was, as far as he was concerned, more beautiful than Cyrene. Jerusalem. Which is how we came to be there on that day. The trip.

I grew up hearing about the trip. 'Alexander,' my father used to say to me, 'when we make the trip we will see wonderful things and places, we will see Alexandria, founded three hundred years ago by your namesake.'

Now, these days my father is rather frail, he has to be careful, his heart is not too good. But in those days he was all muscle. Big, powerful. A laughing, simple man, every inch a farmer, but when he spoke of the trip he became a dreamer. The trip was to spend Passover, just once, in Jerusalem. To pray in the Temple, to make an offering, to see the lovely buildings. Jerusalem was about a thousand miles away. As far as we, a farmer's family, were concerned, it might have been a million. The trip was something we grew up with, we grew up hearing about. It was my father's dream, a sort of family joke. But once, when Rufus and I were in our teens, and much given to scoffing, my mother said, 'No dream; no joke. Your father wants this thing; it will come to pass.' And a year or two later it did. We were astonished. We made the trip. We went overland, we joined the great trade caravans, we saw Alexandria. And Pelusium, and Gaza. It took a long time, but my father had planned well. We found a little house to rent in the pretty country near Bethlehem, about five miles south of Jerusalem. Rufus and I spent the week before the Passover exploring and seeing all we could. So much to see. The Golden City of Solomon and Herod. The gorgeous Temple; the palaces; the changing of the Procurator's Roman Guard; the Tower of Antonia; the Hippodrome and the theatres.

We listened as well as looked. We understood everything. In Jerusalem the Jews speak both Aramaic and Greek, as here. There seemed to be a lot of excitement in the city; a lot of talk of 'Jesus the Carpenter', the 'Miracle-worker', the 'Healer', the 'great Preacher'. We heard about him everywhere. Marvellous stories. From all sorts of people. We took it all home to father. He listened, and said, 'Yes, I've also heard of him. Don't believe all you hear. And go to bed early. I want to be in the city at daybreak. There will be thousands.'

He was right. First day of Passover and day before Sabbath. Big day. Mother stayed home, busy. But we were there; showing off our new knowledge to Dad. He was full of wonder. Everywhere huge crowds. Excitement. Then, suddenly we were in a different sort of excitement, absolutely unexpected. Round a corner came a screaming mob. In front,

a square of Roman soldiers, one of them carrying a roughly
painted sign saying 'King of the Jews'. We thought for a
moment that it was a parade, a carnival. Then we saw inside
the square a man bent under the weight of a huge wooden
cross. He looked ghastly. He was deathly white and covered
in blood. As we looked, he staggered and fell and the cross
banged down on him. The soldier in charge shouted at him
to get up but he couldn't. The soldier looked round into the
crowd, drew his shortsword, and came over to my father.
'You look strong,' he said. 'Carry the cross.' My father started
to explain that we were tourists, pilgrims. 'Doesn't matter,'
said the soldier. 'Roman law. You're pressed into service.
Pick it up. You don't get a choice.' And he whacked my
father, not hard, as part of the law, with the flat of the sword.
My father started to lose his temper but the man on the
ground was looking up at him. It was a calm look. Very tired.
My father went across and bent down and shouldered the
cross. It was obviously heavy. With his free hand he helped
the man to his feet and held him up. It was Jesus, although
at that moment we didn't know it. The soldiers got into
position again and the procession moved off again.

It was quite a long way. We walked along by the soldiers.
Once or twice I made a sign to my father that I would take
my turn with the cross (I was as big and strong as he was)
but he shook his head and went on. I remember he looked
rather proud. Jesus staggered along almost without a word.
Once he stopped and spoke to some women who were weeping
as they walked with him, but the soldiers got rough with both
him and the crowd.

When we reached the place called Golgotha – the Hill of
the Skull – the officer in charge talked to my father for a
while and the soldiers took the cross away. Rufus and I wanted
to stay but my father said no. He said no in a way that we
never argued with. He is a mild man, my father, but like steel
on some things.

'We will not stay,' he said. 'A man, that man, is to be
stripped naked and nailed to that cross with iron spikes

through his hands and feet. The cross is then to be stood up and dropped into a hole so that it stands upright. The man is nearly dead with one of the worst floggings I've ever seen, his skin hangs like rags. He is neither criminal nor traitor. He is a poor preacher. If this can happen in Jerusalem,' said my father, 'on the Passover, this is no place for us. We go home tomorrow. The trip is over.'

The End

❖◆❖◆❖◆❖◆❖◆❖◆❖◆❖◆❖◆❖◆❖◆❖◆❖◆❖◆❖◆❖◆❖◆❖◆❖◆

RUFUS

*Ex-soldier. Middle sixties. Medium build, upright, trim,
muscular. A widower, living alone. A sad, indrawn expression. A lonely man, with memories. The slow speech
of a man by habit silent for long periods. Well respected
in his village.*

This little village is a nice place to live. People in the main
mind their own business. A man earns his living, does his job,
and is left alone. I'm a sort of celebrity for something I'm
ashamed of; for something I'd rather forget; and the village
knows it and doesn't mention it. We are all Christians in the
village. Me, too. But twenty years ago, when they crucified
Jesus, no one was. Well, there was no such thing. I was told
that you went to hear him and he gave you a sort of simple
way of looking at things. Food for thought. It was after he
was dead that the disciples really began to work at making
what he'd said into a religion. Terrible death he had.

People say that he knew what was going to happen; that
it was all in the Scriptures. That he was a prophecy come
true. Well, maybe. But I'm sure there was nothing in the
Scriptures about how we dressed him up and made fun of
him and how we jeered at him and insulted him. All right,
soldiers can get rough – especially with a convicted law-
breaker, but we were *really* rough. I wish to God I could say
I hadn't joined in. But I did. I don't know who first thought
of dressing Jesus up to look like a king, but it seemed very
funny at the time. None of our platoon was at the sort of
trial they gave him. All we knew was that he was a troublemaker who'd gone around saying he was King of the Jews.

We knew very little. We were a Roman garrison. Our orders came from Pilate. Pontius Pilate. The orders were clear. A scourging and crucify him with two other criminals.

Not many people have seen a Roman punishment scourge. It's one of the worst whips ever invented. It can kill a man. It's designed to break skin and wrap round and tear. I've been asked why scourge a man who's going to be killed the same morning. Well, it wasn't the first time – and Pilate was hard. Also, he was fed up with the whole business. I didn't do the whipping, a great big sergeant from Syria did that, but I put the robe on. One of the lads found it somewhere. A purple robe, to make Jesus *look* like a king. When we put it on him, he looked like a corpse. He was naked, and that sergeant knew his job. Jesus could hardly stand. His back was like raw meat. I often dream of it. One of the boys had made a crown of twisted-together thorn stalks and he forced it down on Jesus's head. More blood. Then we stood him on a vegetable basket and marched round him and bowed and saluted and shouted in his face – and when his head dropped we slapped it up again. We gave him a big onion for an orb and a twig for a sceptre and we spat at him and laughed till we were weak. Till we cried.

I've cried many times since. In my sleep mostly. I can't say that the shame began right away, it didn't. As a soldier you do many things that you wouldn't in civilian life. But out of the service, by yourself, with time to look back, you see things differently. About eight years ago, when I'd been demobbed about a year, I met Peter the Fisherman, who made me a Christian. I was in a bad way and told him all about that night and my shame. Peter listened and then said, 'I know about shame. On that night he was a stranger to you, a nothing, to be made sport of. On that night I'd known him three years and believed him to be the Son of God. I was his first follower and his friend. Yet on that night, in fear, I denied that I knew him. Three times.'

I think Peter said it to comfort me. It did a bit. But not much. Nothing does very much. You know, I haven't talked about that night for years. I think of it often; I dream about it, but I don't often talk about it. It's strange how talking about it somehow loosens the memory. All sorts of other things come back. As I told you, my feeling of shame about joining in that night didn't begin till some time after. We were a rough lot. We were Roman occupation troops and we regarded the convicted prisoner as fair game. It broke the monotony.

So did a crucifixion. We didn't like the job but if we were detailed that was it. Our duties were clear. There were regulations; a rulebook. The crosses were ordered normally three at a time – because normally three criminals were done together. There used to be a joke, made first, I was told, by Pilate. Seems he said, 'Do 'em in threes, nice company for each other.' It's possible; he was a cruel, hard man, was Pilate, with jokes to match. The prisoner carried his own cross, or at least dragged it with the cross bar over his shoulder. Very heavy the crosses were. A long, up-and-down, winding route would be worked out, so that as many people as possible would see the prisoner and read his crime, written on a board and carried by the lead corporal. Jesus's board just said 'King of the Jews'. Another Pilate joke. When the Jewish elders asked him to change it, he refused and got very nasty.

Jesus was too weak to carry his cross. Not surprising, he'd been flogged half to death, so we pressed into service a man in the crowd. It was regulations; he couldn't refuse. There were regulations for everything. The distance apart of the crosses, the nailing of the hands and feet, the periods of watch, the crowd control, everything. There were also certain perks. Extra pay, extra drink ration – it could be a bloody business, the nailing part – and extra leave the following week. Also, we were entitled to the clothes and possessions of the prisoners. We would settle who got what by casting lots or gambling. Jesus had no possessions, and his clothes and sandals were poor stuff. We did better out of the two criminals we hung with him. They made a lot of noise those two, shouting and screaming, sometimes sensibly, sometimes like crazy or drunk men.

There were always women who offered drugged wine to those on the cross. Sisters of mercy. It was allowed in regulations. Jesus refused. He didn't say much. At one point I think he said a few words of comfort to the fellow on his left. There were some women a little way off who seemed to know him. None of his followers or disciples was there. They were all lying low, in hiding, out of sight. We put the three prisoners up at nine in the morning. Fine, sunny morning. But at noon the sun went in and it got darker and darker. And very still and close. Most unusual. Frightening. Never before, or since. At about three o'clock all three had been quiet for some time. They'd been up six hours. Suddenly Jesus raised his head and looked up at the sky. I was quite near. Then he shouted at the top of his voice. His face was alight, his voice and body full of power. It was impossible. The crowd, in the weird twilight, were scared and nervous. My mates moved in a bit. Then Jesus shouted again, with the same lift of the head, the same power. 'It is finished!' he shouted. He died magnificently. I've never seen anything like it. One of the things that got him hung was saying he was the Son of God. At that moment I believed he was. I've believed it ever since.

AYALA

About thirty. A well-made, handsome woman. Dark hair and eyes, which are rather sad. The smile is beautiful, but rarely seen. A throaty, rather rough voice. Poorly dressed, but with a certain style.

My mother-in-law, who lives with me, would probably tell you that her Josh didn't deserve what he got, that he was the most marvellous son in the world, as good as gold. He wasn't. He used to hit her sometimes. His father did, and Josh grew up, I reckon, thinking that's how you treat women. It's how he treated me. Not all the time, but often enough.

I don't really know what 'getting what you deserve' means. Josh was a thief, and he was violent. Sometimes he would hurt people when he took things away from them. One day he killed somebody and he was caught and executed. 'Nailed' as he called it. On the cross. I don't know whether anybody 'deserves' that sort of death. I suppose if you were to kill somebody by nailing them up with great iron nails through their hands and feet and leaving them to hang in the sun, *then* you might deserve the same.

Josh was wicked, and very strong, and he drank too much – and had a terrible temper. But it was over in a minute. I bet the man he killed was dead in a minute. Still, as I say, I don't really know how to think about such things.

That's Josh. What about me? After all, I was his wife, I knew he was a thief. I wasn't proud of it, but I didn't stop him (no one could stop him doing *any*thing!). So what about *me*? Surely *I* 'deserve' some punishment too? All right, I'm a widow, but it's the first peace of mind – and body – I've known for years. A 'bereaved mother' lives with me, but we get on well. She remembers Josh a bit rosier than I do, but, if she's honest, *her* life is better now, too. And my daughter is the prettiest ten-year-old in the street, with her father's looks, but only his looks. And now he's gone, his influence is gone. She'll be something, my Ruth. Something more than if Josh had lived. Call things by their right names, my father used to say, and that's what I'm doing.

It would be very funny if, after all the thieving and the hurting people and the murder, Josh is in fact not in Hell but in Paradise, like the Carpenter promised.

He and the Carpenter were executed on the same day. Four years ago next Friday. I'm a follower of the Carpenter, I belong to the Fellowship. Anybody can. It doesn't matter what Josh was. My mother-in-law laughs at me, she says I'm trying to keep on the good side of the Carpenter so he'll keep his promise to Josh. Well, maybe. It wasn't *all* bad with my thieving husband. There were some good times. Not many, but they were very good. We were in the middle of one when he was arrested. I should have known, with him staying at home more than usual, that he'd done something bad.

There was a sort of trial, but only to sentence him. He was guilty; he did it. He was in prison about three weeks before that Friday. There's no appeal against the sentence — except to Governor Pilate, and that would have been a waste of time. He's a terrible, cruel, man. Since the Carpenter, even worse.

We could take food, but not talk to Josh. On the day before the execution we were told the route, and where we could stand. Walking along by the prisoners was not allowed, in case of disturbance. We stood on a corner with four soldiers keeping an eye on us. We waited for hours. One of the soldiers said there would be two prisoners, Josh and another man, who'd also killed somebody. But when the prisoners came along the road, there was a third man. The crowds were shouting his name. Jesus, of Nazareth. The Carpenter. I knew him. Everyone knew him. Not that you would have recognized him. He was covered in blood, with a sort of hat made of spiky twigs pushed down on his head. He looked awful. As far as I could see, Josh and the other man had not been ill-treated at all.

Nearly all on our corner were women and most of us were in tears, some of us very noisy. I think I was more sorry for the Carpenter than for Josh. He looked half-dead — and what could he have done? He was a *preacher*!

As the soldiers and the three prisoners drew near to us, the wailing and crying got louder. Not just from our corner, but from both sides of the street. Hundreds of women. Jesus stopped a minute and spoke to us, of sad times to come, of what men do to each other (he was a good example). 'If this is what they do when the wood is green,' he said, 'what will they do when it is seasoned?'

It was as though he had spoken to me, because before Josh went to the bad he worked as a treefeller, for his uncle, who's got a timber yard. I knew about green wood and seasoned wood. Funny, isn't it?

One of the soldiers pushed him, and the party passed us. Josh and the other man – called Theo, I knew him, a foul-mouthed bully – were dragging their own crosses. The Carpenter's was being dragged by a man who looked as though he'd just been pulled from the crowd. A pilgrim, or tourist (it was holiday time). Poor Jesus didn't look as if he could carry a twig, let alone a great heavy wooden cross.

We were allowed to follow the crowds. The soldiers stayed with us. The place of execution is called the Hill of the Skull. The crosses were laid down. The stripping of the men, and the nailing, was done right away, quickly, with the crowd kept back. Fancy wanting to see it. But people do. The worst part was when the crosses, with the men on, were upended and dropped into their holes. The holes were deep. I shall never forget the sound.

Once the crosses were up, we were allowed nearer. I went behind, I couldn't look at the men. Josh hung like a broken doll. He'd fainted, I think, when the cross had dropped into the hole. There was no life in any of them. The Carpenter was in the worst state. He looked as though he'd been flogged half to death.

Then the mob started. Nearly everyone had heard the stories about the Carpenter being the Messiah, and the Son of God, and about his miraculous cures, and how he had saved lives. Not everyone believed the stories. The mob in general believes nothing. I know; I'm one of them. Or was.

The jokers in the mob were shouting for Jesus to save his own life if he was so clever, if he could do such miracles. And how come his Father, God, was letting him get nailed? And, if he was the Messiah, how come he was on the cross between two murderers?

Then the soldiers who'd been the escort, and had done the nailing and putting up, piled all the clothes together and started to gamble for them. It's traditional. It says in the Scriptures that the hung are the damned and their belongings are anybody's. I learnt that at Fellowship.

I went round to the side after a while. Nothing happens, you see. It's only waiting. The sun was high. Three black crosses with three naked men on them. Dying. You just wait.

All three of them seemed to wake up at the same time. The other man, Theo, started to scream like an animal, waving his head, using terrible language. The Carpenter heard the mob's remarks and seemed to be praying. Josh was still, turning his head carefully, licking his lips, looking for me. I was only about six yards away. I moved round to the front, closer to him. A woman made a remark about his body and I clouted her. Josh heard me and caught my eye. He nodded, and tried to smile. He approved of clouting, my thief did.

Suddenly Theo stopped shouting nonsense and started to direct his filthy words at the Carpenter. He didn't get far. Josh found his voice, told him to shut up, to do a bit of praying instead. 'What are you going on about?' he said. 'You're getting what you deserve, like me, but this man never did anything wrong in his life.'

Jesus turned his head. Above his head was a bit of board saying 'King of the Jews'. One of Governor Pilate's little jokes. Josh read it out loud and then said, sort of to cheer Jesus up perhaps, 'Jesus,' he said, 'when you come into your Kingdom, will you remember me?'

Then Jesus spoke. He said it. He made the promise. 'I tell you,' he said, 'truly, this very day you will be with me in Paradise.'

Well, there you are. As I said, it would be a funny thing if that's where my thief is. He must have felt very out of place, at first.

EZRI

Seventies. Of medium height, but stooped, and slight. Pale, and with thin, white hair. A sparse beard. A trusting, tentative expression. Slow of speech.

I have very few visitors and am somewhat out of practice in the matter of conversation. You must bear with me. I have a great-nephew, Jonathan, of whom I am very fond. He tries to shock me with the length of his hair, and his highly coloured and unorthodox clothes – and succeeds – but I like him very much. He loves to tell me of the full, eventful life he lives. How he has seen more in seventeen years than I have in seventy. He often asks me whether I feel I've missed a lot by spending my life in the Great Temple. Whether I feel I should have mixed more in what he calls 'the life outside the walls', the life of Jerusalem.

Well, perhaps, although I must admit that I was never attracted to the life outside. I am rather shy, and of a somewhat weak and timid nature. My father understood me very well and did not suggest that I follow any profession other than his own. A servant of the Temple. My two elder brothers, alas, both dead, were strong men, full of ambition and drive, and wanted nothing of the Temple. My father did not complain, one son to follow him was enough, as he followed his father, and his father, his.

It is difficult to find words to answer Jonathan, although he is well brought up and listens with respect, but, you know, to live and work in the Temple is not to be 'imprisoned'; it is to live among beauty and be close to God. Great Herod did many terrible things, but he also rebuilt the Temple – and he knew about beauty. His sons were not to be compared, or the Roman procurators, Gratus, Pilate, any of them. They did not care about the Temple.

And we are not so shut off, so cloistered. It is not a monastery, it is a wonder of the world, to which hundreds of thousands of people come each year. The world *outside* comes *in*. Once it came in in a way that changed my life..Not my *way* of life, my *mind*. I still serve, although I do less because I am old, but my *mind* is in some way changed. I don't often speak of it, but Pontius Pilate was recalled to Rome two weeks ago. And will not return. And my thoughts go back.

It does not seem like seven years ago. Passover time. I think it used to be my favourite time of the year. Until that year. So much trouble that year. We seemed to hear of nothing but the Galilean, the Carpenter, Jesus of Nazareth. High Priest Caiaphas seemed to be in a temper the whole time. On the Sabbath the procession of the Sanhedrin and elders seemed to be full of worried, tense faces. The Carpenter was a great disturbance. He seemed to have no fear. When he and his followers overturned all the money changers' stalls that time, there was nearly a riot. I never met him and never saw him. I would have liked to, I think. Many of his sayings and the way he put things in his teaching were collected by one of my colleagues, who is a scholar with a great regard for simplicity. In his opinion the Galilean had a great gift, both for simplicity and for picturesque parable. Certainly he seemed by his words to be a simple and honest man. Yes, I would have liked to have known him. But it was quite forbidden for us of the Inner Courts to attend any outside meetings.

Like my father before me, I am what is called a Servant of the Inner Courts. The Inner Courts surround the Holy Place, the Holy of Holies, where no man enters. We who serve the Inner Courts are all Levite, all of the direct line of Aaron, brother of Great Moses. As I said, I do very little these days. I am neither so strong nor, to be honest, so reliable. I forget things, or do them twice. Seven years ago, before the Passover, I did more. I had various duties, including the care of the gold and silver lamps and ornaments, but my work stopped at the great curtain that enclosed and covered the entrance to the Holy of Holies. I spent hours looking at that curtain. It was gorgeous. The work of a hundred women. My late wife was one. It was blue and purple and crimson, with a design of angels and cherubim in the most exquisite embroidery. Gorgeous. But strong also. Made to conceal; and to last. The finest linen, lined and thickened. Edged and strengthened. It hung, on golden rings, from a great rail. It was lit from above, with great clarity, by daylight. The blue sky and the sunshine of Israel.

Yet, seven years ago, on the first day of Passover, at noon, the blue sky turned dark and the sun went out. At a time of the year when the sun is always there, it suddenly wasn't there. An awful stillness began; a terrible feeling of silence, of foreboding. I realized that I had carried the feeling within me since I'd woken up that morning. As the darkness increased, I knew why. I knew that up on the Hill of the Skull, on Golgotha, Jesus was on the cross. Everyone knew. I carried on with my work. It got darker. Too dark to work. I sat and looked at my beloved curtain, which seemed to glow in the gloom.

The time passed. At about three o'clock the closeness and silence became almost unbearable, and then a terrifying rumbling began deep in the ground, which began to shake and move. Then there was thunder, and lightning. I could hear things falling and people screaming. I think I heard a great shout, by one voice. I was full of terror. As I staggered to my feet, there was a sudden pause, a hush. And then the curtain tore. From top to bottom. A violent, dreadful destruction, full of a sort of anger, of despair.

I was told later that there was no damage either to the walls at the side of the curtain or to the great rail it hung from. I was told also that at three o'clock, Jesus shouted, and died.

The Beginning

❖❖❖❖❖❖❖❖❖❖❖❖❖❖❖❖❖❖❖❖❖❖❖❖❖❖❖❖❖❖

ZEKE

*Middle fifties. Powerfully built and weather-beaten.
Deep-set, rather humorous eyes. Grizzled hair, big eyebrows. A deep, slightly hoarse, voice. A cheerful man.*

It was an odd feeling, you know, to change jobs so late in
life, after so many years. Very different jobs indeed – although
still a council employee. A bath attendant, instead of a cemetery attendant. Swimming pool instead of graveyard. Surrounded every day by noisy people full of health, instead of
dead people – who made no noise at all!

Except one. He didn't so much make a noise as *cause* a lot
of noise and disturbance – and got me the sack! Although
I'm not really complaining. To be honest, I like this job
better. After that Sunday I prefer the living to the dead. I
didn't always.

Councillor Joseph, of Arimathea, got me this job. Nice
man. Said it was the least he could do after helping me lose
the last one. I'm not sure what he means; it wasn't his fault.
I don't know whose fault it was, really. But not his, the grave
was his own property, he could do what he liked with it. No
regulations broken.

Regulations. Doing things the right way. I believe in that.
I've got no education – you don't need to be clever to work
in a graveyard – but I know that things should be done right.
It may be that I'm superstitious, but you don't bury a gallows
body in a rich man's tomb. The hung are damned. It's written.
In any case the damned and the stoned and the crucified
have their own graveyard. Near the quarry. Pits, as is right.
You don't put them in newly built tombs, with closing stones.

It was bad enough the graveyard being right next door to the crucifixion hill. People used to picnic on the graves, or leave their children with me whilst they went to watch the executions. I didn't mind, I like children, but the graveyard used to get very untidy, and I like order. Things should be tidy, and in their place.

If Councillor Joseph's friend had stayed 'in his place', I think I'd still be working up there! Lucky the wife's not with me, she doesn't like jokes of that sort. In any case, she says she knew the Councillor's friend – and even a marble tomb in the Temple wouldn't have been good enough for him! Women, bless 'em.

I spoke of the Sunday; the whole weekend was strange. What is it, about a year and a half? I remember it like yesterday. In some ways the Friday was more frightening than the Sunday, a thousand times more.

It started normally. Nice morning. Cool, fresh, usual for Spring. The usual one or two early-morning people, visiting graves. One of them told me there'd been a lot of noise in the city during the night. At the palace, at the High Priest's house – and at the praetorium, where Governor Pilate lives.

There was to be a crucifixion, he told me. Three, in fact. Very unexpected, that, on a Friday – and, if I remember rightly, it was the first day of Passover, too. Almost before he finished telling me, I saw the crowds coming up the hill. It was no more than eight o'clock. Three crosses being carried. I remember thinking 'somebody's in a hurry to cross them off!' (Don't tell the wife I said that.)

I got on with my work. I don't hold with crucifixion – or the people who go and watch. On crucifixion days I would plant flowers, and look after the dwarf trees and bushes – most of which I put in.

That day I was working on the Councillor's tomb. A nice piece of work. Cut into a natural rock outcrop up at the higher end of the cemetery – away from the crucifixion end, luckily. I was lining the little trench which guides the closing stone with pebbles, so that when it rolls across, on edge, it doesn't sink in. Those closing stones can be very heavy. I've seen as many as twenty mourners needed to move one. End of the service; male relatives and friends to the stone. The wealthier the man, the bigger the stone. Councillor Joseph is very wealthy.

I set pebbles and put in little plants. I occupied myself. From down the slope I could hear the crowd making mob noises. Nasty.

It began to get terribly close, and hot. And silent. I didn't notice it at first, but I like birds, and enjoy their song – and suddenly I was aware the birds had stopped. It was uncanny. Then I noticed the sky starting to change colour. It went red, like anger, then purple. Then dark grey – then black! At noon! I was on my knees. As I got to my feet I felt the ground move. I thought it was *me*, that I was fainting – that it was *my* things 'going black'.

It wasn't. The earth *was* moving, with awful rumbling, grinding, crushing noises. I could hear people screaming and crying. I lay down and hid my head in my arms. No hero, me.

It went on and on, seemingly for hours. Then it stopped, and it began to get light again. It was about three o'clock. I was stiff. I got up and walked around the graveyard to see what damage had been done. At first I could see nothing at all. None of the upright headstones, which you'd think would be flat, were different in any way.

Then I saw a very scary thing. One of the ordinary graves, with the headstone upright and tidy, looked as if it had burst open; as if the body had burst out – and gone! It gave me a funny feeling. There were about four like it. The earth pushed violently up and thrown to either side – as though from *inside*!

I decided that I would fill them in again in a day or two (they scared me) and went back to the Councillor's tomb, which was the same as before. Everything was; sunshine, breeze, birdsong, everything. When I got there, the Councillor was waiting. I was surprised. He looked very white and strained. He told me to get the tomb ready and cleaned for someone who had just died. 'I will go and get permission, from Governor Pilate,' he said. When I looked puzzled – for a Jewish cemetery is nothing to do with the Romans – he said, 'It's one of the three men just crucified,' and walked away, looking very choked up.

Well, I thought, none of my business, and I got busy. Most unusual. As I said, there are pits. That cemetery is rather a smart one. Titled people, upper-income groups. Old families, family tombs. Now, in a brand new, cut-from-the-solid-rock, rich man's vault – with a huge closing stone – we were to put to rest a felon, a convicted and executed law-breaker. I was quite put out by it.

The body was brought in the late afternoon, by some of the Councillor's servants, who were told to come back a bit later to help move the stone across. I looked around for the embalmers, but the Councillor told me that he and a friend called Nicodemus (I know him, his parents are buried there) would prepare the body themselves. They did it well, too. I've seen the best. No expense spared, the finest linen, the purest myrrh and aloes – about a hundred pounds of it! Fit for a king.

We laid the body in, said the prayers, and called the servants back. With the Councillor and Nicodemus, it took fourteen of us to put that stone in place.

The next day, the Sabbath, another surprise. A lot of coming and going of the High Priest's people, and the Temple authorities – and a lot of instructions. All in a 'my man' tone, as the wife calls it. 'You must be very watchful for any suspicious characters near the tomb, my man.' 'The stone is not to be touched in any way, my man.' 'We will be sealing the tomb, my man – and mounting a guard, my man.' A guard! for a dead felon! They meant it, too. Potter's clay sealing, and ten men with two officers. Well, I did my day's work, was 'watchful' and went home, leaving the soldiers to it. The only 'suspicious characters' seen had been some very sad-looking women, probably relations.

When I got to the cemetery the next morning (I don't hurry on Sundays), the place near the tomb had to be seen to be believed. All the soldiers either asleep or just sitting, as though in shock, the stone pushed right back – and the tomb empty! Well, I can't tell you the commotion that went on that day! And the stories that started to fly around!

My day ended with the sniffiest of the Burial Committee sending for me and telling me that the cemetery was to be closed till further notice, that my watchfulness left a lot to be desired, that great confusion and disturbance existed, for which as 'custodian' I had partly to accept responsibility – and, because of all these factors et cetera and so on, I was sacked.

I wasn't too upset. Neither was the wife. Especially as the Councillor fixed me this new job almost the same week. Anyway, the wife thinks a swimming pool's got more class than a cemetery. Certainly more cheerful – and I never had to fill in those graves. Good thing too, seemingly, for a lot of folk swear that the people who were in them have been seen around the city! Peculiar, the whole business. It was in my mind to ask the Councillor how he felt about the tomb being interfered with, and his friend's body disappearing – and all that expensive embalming stuff being wasted – but I didn't. He didn't seem too upset. In fact, he seemed happier than for a long time.

MARON

About twenty-two. Slim, handsome, fair. A well-brought-up, innocent, look. A 'good-school' voice. A sort of fledgling authority. Pleasant.

I'm perfectly willing to tell you all I know about the night the preacher's body went from the tomb, but all I know doesn't amount to very much. I know what I've been told – and it may be the truth – although those who told me weren't even there.

My wife says I worry about it too much. She says it often. She also says that, if it hadn't been for that night, we couldn't have afforded to get married and buy this little house. It's true. Second lieutenants earn almost nothing in the Temple Guards. It's all honour and glory. All father-to-son, if you're an officer. The men do better than we do.

It's very father-to-son in our family. We've been soldiers for generations – right back to Judas Maccabeus. 'More medals than money,' my mother says. She's also very pleased the money came my way, like my wife is. Women have a special sort of logic, I think. My father, who's Household Cavalry attached to Antipas's palace in Tiberias, has made it clear that he won't discuss the matter with me. He sees it as sleeping on duty, and that's the end of it. He's not easy to talk to at any time, my father. My brother, who's a major in the Infantry, is no better. He says it's the highest paid worst bit of soldiering in history. D'you wonder I worry about it? Another thing, my father and my brother are military; they deal with senior officers, the Cavalry and the Infantry. I get my orders from priests. The Temple Guard are really policemen. Our authority comes from the elders, the Sanhedrin Council, the religious parties.

That's where the order came from that Saturday morning. The officers of the High Priest Caiaphas, and the Pharisee Party. It's just over a year ago (we've been married about seven months). The order was simple and clear. A ten-man guard detail with two officers to proceed to the burial ground alongside Crucifixion Hill and mount a day and night guard on a tomb. Not a guard of honour; normal dress and arms. Not a lying-in-state guard; a watch guard. No details given at all as to occupant of the tomb, whose owner was Councillor Joseph of Arimathea, my father's second cousin. Uncle Joseph, who was very much alive.

We were up at the tomb by noon. When we arrived, two

men from Temple maintenance were sealing the front stone
with clay – and attaching the official tags. Seemed a needless
procedure. They were sticking bits of clay round the edge of
a slab of stone that looked as though it weighed fifty tons. It
closed the entrance to the tomb, which was cut in solid rock.
Official sealing, official tags – and a full Temple Guard.
Somebody – or something – very valuable in there, my corporal said.

We sorted out our roster and settled in. Two hours on,
four off. Always four men on guard, officers to share duty.
A sunny, mild afternoon, a cool evening, a cold night. Normal
for the time of year. As I say, what did actually happen I
can't tell you – mainly because I was asleep. It was just before
dawn. I'd done the third night watch and was off duty,
asleep. What woke me was a mixture of things really. A
blinding white light and men shouting in terror. My men,
I'm not proud to tell you. There was a sound like a great
wind, and a movement in the ground, like an earthquake –
or landslide. I was dazed. As I tried to get to my feet, my
corporal, in full flight, with his eyes staring out of his head,
went straight into me.

We both hit the ground together. I caught his fear. I've
never been so frightened – or known less why. I felt some
great thing was happening, to do with the blinding light and
the earth movement. The corporal and I clung together, then
he went limp. I thought he had died of fright! I remember
that just as I thought that such a thing is impossible – everything went dark and *I* fainted! It couldn't have been for long.
It seemed, as I came to, that the whole troop was waking up.
I got up to investigate, feeling very groggy. Zephah, the other
officer, was as unsteady on his feet as I was. The great white
light had gone. It was a pale dawn.

You know, sometimes you just don't believe what your
eyes tell you. The stone had been rolled right back! Right
back, as though it weighed a penny. Rolled on edge – *like* a
penny! Not a lever, or a footmark, or a clue of any kind.
The tomb was empty – except for some body wrappings. If

there had been valuables – it was a rich man's tomb – they'd gone.

Zephah and I got much the same thought at the same moment. Court-martial. Twelve men guarding one small place against God knows what – and failing completely.

We questioned the men together. They all seemed dazed, in shock, stupid. Or drugged. There'd been a lot of talk lately in the city, of students inducing 'mind journeys' or 'trips' with hallucination drugs, and it occurred to me that our wine or water or food had been tampered with. The men's stories varied a lot but had certain things in common. All spoke of the brilliant light. Two said it was a man, or two men, who gave off the light. An angel, one said; the other, a 'white-hot' man. No one had seen anybody move the stone or leave the tomb. Some spoke of music from the sky, of great singing winds, or choirs. Others, of shooting stars, and explosions in their heads, and powerless limbs, and terror. Others still, of the stone 'leaping' to one side, and great groans from the bowels of the earth, great weeping noises from Heaven. All told of everything going black, of fainting, of terror, of collapse.

Zephah and I talked. We were in trouble. What could we report? If we wrote down what the men had told us, it would look like the burblings of lunatics – or men crazy-drunk. It would do nothing to hide the simple fact that the thing which we were there to prevent had happened. It was our fault. We were officers in charge. The blame was ours.

We decided to go ourselves to Council, and tell all we knew. We went first to tell our C.O., who went glassy-eyed, for our absolute failure of duty was certain to reflect upon him. He came with us to the Temple.

We told our story first to the elders, who sat like statues, then we went with them to the palace of High Priest Caiaphas, and repeated it all to him. He has an unblinking stare, Caiaphas, and eyes with no expression. Terrifying. When we'd finished, he nodded and told us to wait in a small ante-room. We were in that room about two hours, shaking, for dereliction of duty carries not only disgrace to the whole family, but punishment of a most severe kind.

Then we were called back in. Just the two of us, not our C.O. We were spoken to by one of the elders, I believe a cousin of Caiaphas, with a smooth, modulated voice – and the same eyes. He told us that we had been the victims of a diabolically clever plot, in which powerful drugs, magic and sorcery had been used to make powerless twelve highly trained men to whom no blame could be in any way attached. Indeed, he said, we were to be richly rewarded for our bravery – and discretion.

When I looked puzzled about the word discretion, he went on to tell us that he could now reveal that the body in the tomb had been that of the Galilean preacher, Jesus. The Carpenter. The fraud and impostor crucified for his crimes against the people and sedition against Rome. Tried and sentenced by Governor Pilate himself. The tomb had been sealed and guarded against a foreseen attempt by the dead preacher's followers to make the body disappear as though by a miracle and thus perpetuate the fraud and deception of the people. All was foreseen, he told us, and allowed for. No shame or dishonour; a reward. And that was the story. The only story. No other. Even if Governor Pilate himself were to ask us, that was the story. Drugs, magic and sorcery, and the stealing of the body by a large gang of trained agitators.

Then the elder gave us a bag of gold to share among the men, and a bag of gold each for ourselves, nearly as big. Before distributing the money to the men, the elder said, explain to them – and teach them – the exact, and only, story.

And that's it. You needn't tell me the other stories, of the Carpenter rising from the dead and meeting his friends and so on, I've heard them. Good luck to him. I'm grateful to him. Because of him I'm married, and we've got a nice little house and garden. As my wife says to tell you, if you don't like one story, choose another, there are lots.